Grade 2

Scott Foresman

Read Aloud

Anthology

Scott Foresman
is an imprint of

Glenview, Illinois • Boston, Massachusetts • Chandler, Arizona
Upper Saddle River, New Jersey

Pearson® is a trademark, in the U.S. and/or in other countries, of Pearson plc or its affiliates.
Scott Foresman® is a trademark, in the U.S. and/or in other countries, of Pearson Education, Inc., or its affiliates.

2 3 4 5 6 7 8 9 10 V031 13 12 11 10

ISBN 13: 978-0-328-47666-4
ISBN 10:   0-328-47666-8

Contents

Unit 1 Exploration

Unit 2 Working Together

Unit 3 Creative Ideas

Unit 4 Our Changing World

Unit 5 Responsibility

Unit 6 Traditions

Movin' On In

BY TAYLOR JORDAN

"Beecher Bees are great because
Beecher Bees have got the BUZZ!"

The crowd cheered. It was the last game of the school year—and it was a win!

"Good game, Beecher!" yelled Cara.

"Way to go, Bees!" shouted Anna.

Cara grabbed her Bee backpack. Anna zipped up her Bee sweatshirt.

"Come on!" Cara said. "The bus is leaving."

The twins didn't live in Beecher. They lived in Rockville, the next town over. Rockville was too small to have its own school. So Cara and Anna had gone to Beecher since kindergarten.

But that was about to change.

"No more Beecher buses for your two!" said their neighbor, Mr. Dewey. "Look at this!" He waved his newspaper. "In September, you'll be going to school right here in Rockville."

All summer Cara, Anna, and their friends watched the new school being built.

"They'd better not forget to put in a cafeteria," Ben said. He looked worried. "Lunch is my favorite subject!"

"What if they forget to put in bathrooms?" asked Sophie.

"Maybe they won't finish in time," said Anna.

"Maybe they'll change their minds about having a school at all!" Cara piped up.

"Do you think so?" asked Henry. "I'll keep my fingers crossed."

But Rockville School opened right on time. "It's so—*new*," said Anna, peeking into their classroom.

The desks didn't have any scratches.

The chalkboard was perfectly clean.

Even the floors looked bright and shiny.

"Isn't it nice?" asked Ms. Bean, the Rockville principal. She knew most of the kids because she had taught at Beecher.

"Just think," Cara said. "We'll be the first Rockville students ever!"

A few weeks passed and the kids weren't excited anymore. They just couldn't get used to their new school.

"I keep getting lost in the halls," Cara complained.

"Me, too," said Anna. "And I keep slipping on these new floors," she added.

"There are too many choices in the cafeteria," muttered Ben.

"I almost walked into the boys' bathroom—twice!" said Sophie.

Something else was wrong, too.

"This school doesn't feel like *ours*," said Ben.

"Yeah," Sophie agreed. "It's like we're just visiting or something."

Anna sighed. "I miss being a Beecher Bee."

"Me, too," said Cara.

Everybody nodded.

That night, Cara and Anna had history homework to do. They were studying the American Revolution.

"Isn't this weird?" Anna said. "Even after they fought to be free, some Americans still thought of themselves as English."

"What's weird about that?" Cara asked. "I still feel like a Beecher Bee."

Anna kept reading aloud. "The Founders wanted Americans to feel patriotism—love for their new country. So they chose symbols, like the flag and the bald eagle, to stand for America."

"I get it!" said Cara. "The symbols helped people feel like they belonged."

Anna thought about her Beecher sweatshirt.

Cara thought about her Bee backpack.

"Symbols!" they both blurted out.

"Hey, are you thinking what I'm thinking?" asked Cara.

"Yes!" said Anna. "And we have to tell Ms. Bean about it!"

"Ms. Bean, Rockville needs symbols!" Cara exclaimed the next morning.

"Cymbals? For the band?" Ms. Bean looked puzzled.

"No," said Anna. "Like the bad eagle!"

"You want a class pet?" asked Ms. Bean.

Anna shook her head. "The kids at Rockville are like the first settlers. We like our new school—sort of—but we don't *belong* yet."

"That's why we need stuff to give us school pride!" added Cara. "You know, the way the flag helped people feel proud to be Americans."

"Oh, *symbols!*" laughed Ms. Bean.

Then she looked serious.

"Girls, you're exactly right."

Ms. Bean called everyone into the lunchroom. "Anna and Cara have come up with a terrific suggestion. Rockville needs school symbols—like a team name and school colors and our own cheer."

"Yay! All right!" the kids yelled.

"Let's start with the team name," Ms. Bean went on. "At Beecher, we wee the Bees. What should we be at Rockville? Think of names, and next Tuesday we'll take a vote!"

Nobody talked about anything else for days.

"I think we should be the Rockville Bulldogs," said Henry.

"Or the Rockville Lightning Bolts," suggested Sophie.

"How about the Rockville Roaches?" Ben wriggled his fingers. "That would gross out the other teams!"

"*Eeeww!*" everybody said.

Cara and Anna tried to think of names, too. But they couldn't come up with anything they really liked.

It was the morning of the big vote. Anna was finishing her cereal and reading the answer to the Crater Crunch Quiz.

"Crater Crunch to the rescue!" she yelled. "Hey, Cara! I just got a great idea!"

Cara was halfway out the door. "Tell me about it on the way to school, or we'll be late."

Cara and Anna got to the gym just in time. Kids were already calling out team names.

"There are some interesting choices here," said Ms. Bean. "Shall we vote?"

"Wait! Anna has an idea," Cara said.

"I was thinking," Anna began. "We're the first kids at this school, and the astronauts were the first ones on the moon. So how about the Rockville Astros?"

"Yeah!" said Ben. "Our colors could be silver and white, like a rocket."

"Hey! That's IT!" Henry shouted. "The Rockville Rockets!"

Everybody started whooping and clapping.

"Looks like it's unanimous!" Ms. Bean announced.

The next day the kids started making banners and designs for T-shirts.

Sophie even began working on a school cheer.

For the first time since their new school had opened, nobody was thinking about Beecher.

Everybody was thinking about Rockville.

A few weeks later Rockville played its first basketball game. The crowd was really pumped up.

"Looking good, Rockets!" yelled Cara.

"Yay, Rockville!" shouted Anna.

The twins still thought about Beecher sometimes.

But Cara and Anna loved their new school—even if they did get lost in the halls once in a while!

Gloria Rising

BY ANN CAMERON

My mother was making spaghetti sauce. She said, "Gloria, honey, would you go buy me an onion?"

"Sure," I said. She gave me some money, and I went.

The store was crowded with old people holding tightly to their shopping carts, little kids hollering to their parents for candy, and lots of people staring at shopping lists and blocking the aisles.

I ducked around all the carts and went to the back where the vegetables are. From all the onions in the bin, I took the prettiest—a big round one, light tan and shiny, with a silvery glow to its skin.

I carried it to the express checkout and stood at the end of a very long line.

Next to me there was a giant Berkbee's Baby Food display. It was like a wall of glass, and taller than I am. All the little jars were stacked up to look like a castle, with pennants that said "Baby Power" sticking out above the castle doorways and windows. At the top there was a high tower with a red-and-white flag that said "Berkbee's Builds Better Babies!" I started counting the jars, but when I got to 346, I gave up. There must have been at least a thousand.

The checkout line didn't move. To pass the time, I started tossing my onion from hand to hand. I tried to improve and make my throws harder to catch.

A woman wearing a sky-blue jogging suit got in line behind me. She was holding a cereal box. She smiled at me, and I smiled back.

I decided to show her what a really good catcher I am. I made a wild and daring onion throw.

I missed the catch. The onion kept going, straight for the middle of the baby food castle. The castle was going to fall!

My folks would have to pay for every broken jar! The store manager would kill me. After that, my folks would bring me back to life to tell me things that would be much worse than death.

I was paralyzed. I shut my eyes.

I didn't hear a crash. Maybe I had gone deaf from fright. Or maybe I was in a time warp because of my fear. In fifty years the onion would land and that would be the end of me.

I felt a tap on my shoulder. If I opened my eyes, I would see the store manager and all the broken jars.

I didn't want to see him. I didn't want to know how bad it was.

There came a tap again, right on top of my head.

I heard a woman's voice. "I have your onion."

I opened my eyes. The woman in the jogging suit handed the onion to me.

"Lucky I used to play baseball," she said.

"O-o-o-h," I said. I clutched the onion.

"O-o-o-h," I moaned again.

"You're welcome," was all she said.

She had brown eyes with a sparkle in them, and her hair was in shiny black ringlets. She wore blue-green earrings that hung on tiny gold chains. When she tilted her head, her earrings spun around, and I saw they were the Earth—I mean, made to look like the Earth, jeweled with green continents and blue oceans.

"Your earrings are beautiful," I said.

She smiled. "Some friends got them for me," she said, "to remind me of a trip we made."

When she said "trip," her face started to look familiar, but I didn't know why. Then I remembered.

"I've seen you!" I said. "I saw you on TV!"

She smiled. "Could be."

"And you come from right here in town, but you don't live here anymore." I said.

"That's right," she said.

"And you are—aren't you?—Dr. Grace Street, the astronaut!"

She tilted her head, and the little Earths on both her ears spun round. "That's me," she said.

I was amazed, because I never thought I would meet a famous person in my life, and yet one was right beside me in the supermarket, and I myself, Gloria Jones, was talking to her, all because of my onion throw.

"We learned about the space station in school last year," I said. "You were up there, orbiting the Earth."

"My team and I were there," Dr. Street said.

"What is space like?"

"You know," she said.

"How could I know?" I said.

"We're always in space," Dr. Street said. "We're in space right now."

"Yes," I said, "but what was it like out there, where you went? Out there it must seem different."

"Do you really want to know?" she asked, and I said yes.

"The most awesome part was when we had to fix things on the outside of the station. We got our jobs done and floated in our space suits, staring out into the universe. There were zillions of stars—and space, deep and black, but it didn't seem exactly empty. It seemed to be calling to us, calling us to go on an endless journey. And that was very scary.

"So we turned and looked at Earth. We were two hundred miles above it. We saw enormous swirls of clouds and the glow of snowfields at the poles. We saw water like a giant blue cradle for the land. One big ocean, not 'oceans.' The Earth isn't really chopped up into countries, either. Up there you see it is one great big powerful living being that knows a lot, lot more than we do."

"What does it know?" I said.

"It knows how to be Earth," Dr. Street said. "And that's a lot."

I tried to imagine everything she had seen. It gave me a shiver.

"I wish I could see what you saw," I said. "I'd like to be an astronaut. Of course, probably I couldn't."

Dr. Street frowned. "Why do you say 'Probably I couldn't?'"

"Practically nobody gets to do that," I said.

"You might be one of the people who do," she said. "But you'll never do anything you want to do if you keep saying 'Probably I couldn't.'"

"But maybe I can't!" I protested. I looked down at my onion. I didn't think a very poor onion thrower had a chance to be an astronaut.

Dr. Street looked at my onion too. "It was a good throw—just a bad catch," she said. "Anyhow—saying 'Maybe I can't' is different. It's okay. It's realistic.

"Even 'I can't' can be a good, sensible thing to say. It makes life simpler. When you really know you can't do one thing, that leaves you time to try some of the rest. But when you don't even know what you can do, telling yourself 'Probably I couldn't' will stop you before you even start. It's paralyzing. You don't want to be paralyzed, do you?"

"I just was paralyzed," I said. "A minute ago, when I threw my onion. I didn't enjoy it one bit."

"If you don't want to be paralyzed," Dr. Street said, "be careful what you tell yourself—because whatever you tell yourself you're very likely to believe."

I thought about what she said. "If maybe I could be an astronaut," I asked, "how would I get to be one?"

"You need to do well in school," she said. "And you need to tame your fears. Not get rid of them—just tame them."

The line moved forward suddenly, and we moved up. Maybe the people in line behind us thought Dr. Street and I were mother and daughter having a serious conversation, because they left some space around us.

"So how does a person tame fears?"

"By doing things that are difficult, and succeeding," Dr. Street said. "That's how you learn you can count on yourself. That's how you get confidence. But even then, you keep a little bit of fear inside—a fear that keeps you careful."

The checkout line moved again, and we moved with it.

"Big things are really little," Dr. Street said. "That's a great secret of life."

"How—" I began. But I never got to ask how big things are really little, because I was the first person in line.

The checkout man looked at my onion.

"Young lady, didn't you weight that?" he asked.

"No, sir," I said.

"Go back to Produce and have it weighed."

So I had to go.

"Goodbye," Dr. Street said.

"Goodbye," I said. On the way to Produce, I looked back at her. She was walking toward the exit with her cereal box. I waved, but she didn't notice.

And I could see how little things are really big. Just on account of an onion. I had met an astronaut, and on account of that same onion, I had to stop talking to her.

But how big things are really little I couldn't understand at all.

Mission to Mars

BY FRANKLYN BRANLEY

In the last century, Neil Armstrong became the first person to walk on the Moon. In this century, you may become the first person to walk on Mars.

Your spaceship will be launched from the International Space Station. It will take over six months to travel more than 300 million miles in a curved path from Earth to Mars.

When you reach Mars, you and the other three people in your crew will transfer to the Mars Habitat Lander. It was put into orbit around Mars months ago. It will become your station on Mars.

You get ready to take the Lander down to the surface. Parachutes open to ease the landing. Engines that slow the ship are fired. They kick up big clouds of dust and powder. After months of space travel, you are on Mars.

The Mars Station where you will live for the next several months is part of the Lander. It has sections for living, sleeping, exercising, and storage, and a laboratory for conducting experiments.

Some time ago, cargo ships carrying food, air, and water landed nearby. Your first job is to move some of the supplies from the cargo ships to the Station. Each day the crew uses about 100 pounds of food and water, so tons of it are needed.

Luckily, the gravity on Mars is only one third as strong as the gravity on Earth. The supply packages would be heavy on Earth, but here on Mars you can lift them easily.

Mission to Mars by Franklyn M. Branley. Used by permission of HarperCollins Publishers.

There is air inside the Station for you to breathe, so you don't need to wear your space suit. Soon you are ready for bed. A Martian day is just a bit over 24 hours long, so the day-night cycle is about the same here as it is on Earth. At last you can sleep lying down. During the long journey to Mars, you were in microgravity. There was so little gravity that you did not feel it. There was no up or down. On Mars there is enough gravity for you to lie down to sleep without floating away.

After you get up, you check every part of the Station, including the electric system. Electricity is generated by solar panels and an atomic reactor. You make sure that the water recycler is working. The air inside the Station is also recycled.

Now you are ready to explore Mars.

Long before telescopes and rockets were invented, people already knew at least one thing about Mars: they knew it is a reddish planet. Red reminded people of blood and war, so the Romans named the planet after Mars, the god of war.

Today we know much more about Mars. We have thousands of pictures of the planet, taken by probes and robots. Mars is as dry and dusty as a desert. But we know that long ago Mars had water. There are old riverbeds cut into the Martian rock. A huge flat area may have been an ocean.

There are many extinct volcanoes. One of them is about 15 miles high. It is the highest peak in the solar system and three times as high as Mount Everest, the highest point on Earth.

The Martian atmosphere is much thinner than our atmosphere. Most of it is a gas called carbon dioxide. The planet is cold—about 70 degrees Fahrenheit below zero.

The North and South Poles are even colder—about 175 degrees Fahrenheit below zero. The poles are covered by ice and by white, frozen carbon dioxide.

It never rains on Mars. There is not enough water in the air.

But it is likely that there is water below the surface of the planet. In some places there is a layer of ice. Below the ice there may be liquid water. It seeps out of the walls of a few craters.

You will dig wells to recover the water. It will be one of your first jobs, because the crew needs a lot of water.

You will also need to grow some of your food. Plants are grown in a wet, spongy material that roots can anchor to. It is moisturized with water containing all the chemicals that plants need.

Your mission to Mars is the first of what may become many more. To help future astronauts, it is important for your crew to discover as much as possible about the planet.

You will probably find no Martian soil. The entire planet seems to be covered by a layer of particles as fine as talcum powder. It comes from meteors that crashed into Mars long ago, and from volcanic explosions that threw lava and dust clouds over the whole planet. The dust blows about and settles on the entire Mars Station. You will have to brush it off the solar collectors and make sure it doesn't get inside the space suits.

There are no plants on Mars—no animals, birds, or bugs. Did they exist here long ago? At some time during the history of Mars, living things may have developed on the planet. You will search for clues that let us know.

You will use a Mars Rover to explore the parts of the planet far away from the Station. You will find craters that were dug out when meteorites crashed into Mars. The planet was bombarded by them billions of years ago. Some of them were huge. One of the craters is at least 200 miles across and so long, it would reach from the east coast of the United States to the Rocky Mountains.

As you move about in the Rover, you will gather samples of rock to be taken back to the laboratory. Very likely, some will be 4 billion or 5 billion years old—as old as the solar system.

When you get to Mars, you will find things no one could have imagined. No one knows what may be discovered, and that is one of the main reasons why we want to go there.

After several months of exploration, you get inside the Ascent Vehicle. It was landed on Mars long ago. You fire the engines, and it carries you into Mars orbit.

Then you transfer to the Earth Return Vehicle that will make the long journey back home.

After the Mars mission, some people dream of traveling out beyond the solar system—all they way to the stars. But stars are very far away. It is 26,000,000,000,000 miles to the nearest one. Before such a journey can be made, we'll need new engines. They will have to travel at tremendous speeds for years and years. It will take at least a century to develop them. Maybe your great-grandchildren will travel to the stars.

You will have to stay closer to Earth. You might become an engineer at the Moon Base or the International Space Station. You might even set out on another mission to Mars.

Insects Are My Life

BY MEGAN MCDONALD

The night that Andrew caught the fireflies in a jar, Amanda set them all free.

That was the first real clue that Amanda Frankenstein was crazy about insects. Bugs. Dozens of bugs. Cousins of bugs. Big bugs. Small bugs. Any bugs. All bugs. Creepy bugs. Crawly bugs. Slimy bugs. Climby bugs. Bugs with wings. Bugs that sing.

"How would *you* like to live in a peanut butter jar?" she asked her brother. "Bugs are people too, you know!"

That night, she drew a giant dragonfly on the dinosaur poster in his room. And she slipped her ugliest rubber cockroach under his pillow before bed.

Amanda examined bugs. With her detective kit. Under rocks, hidden on leaves, in sidewalk cracks. She counted eleven different kinds in a single afternoon, including a seven-spotted ladybug.

Amanda collected bugs. Dead ones, of course. The skin of a grasshopper, the shell of a cicada, a perfect pair of dragonfly wings found after a thunderstorm. She collected bug cases. Once she hatched hundreds of tiny praying mantises right in her sock drawer. She collected mosquito bites. She counted twenty-two bites on one leg, and she was proud.

Amanda Frankenstein was a bug's best friend. She always stepped *around* spiderwebs. She hid the flyswatter. She rescued five ants from getting stepped on in the kitchen. She clicked her tongue at bats to confuse them and keep them from eating so many insects.

Amanda dreamed of hanging upside down on the ceiling like a fly. She imagined walking on water as nimbly as a water strider. Once she tried crawling forty miles on all fours, like an ant, and got as far as the backyard fence. "That's how far an ant could walk if it was a person!" she explained when her mother called her inside.

"Find something else to do until dinner, Amanda."

So Amanda watched her favorite movie, *The Fly*, two times in a row.

"My sister, the insect," said her brother. Amanda ignored him. Tonight, he would find her trick ice cube in his milk. The one with the dead fly in the center.

After dark, Amanda opened her window wide and turned on the light so all the night bugs would fly in. She spied a yellow hawk moth, a garden tiger moth, and a lacewing fly. That is, until her mother found out. Thanks to Andrew.

"No bugs in the house, Amanda. When you're old enough to have your own house, you can have all the bugs you want there."

"When I'm all grown up, I'm going to be an entomologist," she told her mother, "and hatch rare butterflies in my living room."

"You can't be *that*," said her brother.

"Then you can't be a dead bone digger either!"

"Paleontologist. They study dinosaurs. Dinosaurs are neat. Bugs are slimy."

"*Insects* are not slimy. Insects are fascinating. Insects are my life!"

Around One Cactus Owls, Bats and Leaping Rats

BY ANTHONY D. FREDERICKS

This is the desert, wild and free,
    A place of sun-baked majesty,
With shifting dunes and rocky edges
    And bushes gripping ancient ledges.
Here stands a cactus, tall and grand,
    A haven for creatures in a waterless land.

This is the cactus.

The prickly cactus with arms raised high
    Was watched by a boy with a curious eye.
"Who could be living on this arid ground?"
    He asked as the breeze tumbled all around.

He observed the giant in the fading light,
    But the critters were resting far from sight.
So he turned and slowly walked away.
    Then the creatures woke to play and prey.

A leaping rat builds a cozy nest
    (A sheltered place for her young to rest)
Beside the cactus tall and grand,
    A haven for creatures in a waterless land.

Around One Cactus by Anthony D. Fredericks, Illustrated by
Jennifer DiRubbio, 2003. Reprinted by permission of Dawn Publications.

A tiny owl with perfect sight,
    Who sleeps by day and hunts by night,
Lives high above her neighbor's nest
    (A special place for young to rest)
Beside the cactus tall and grand,
    A haven for creatures in a waterless land.

A long-nose bat flies to this tower
    And spreads the pollen from flower to flower,
Above the owl with perfect sight,
    Who sleeps by day and hunts by night,
Who lives above her neighbor's nest
    (A special place for young to rest)
Beside the cactus tall and grand,
    A haven for creatures in a waterless land.

A rattlesnake with deadly teeth
    Slips-slides across the ground beneath
The long-nose bat upon the tower,
    Who spreads the pollen from flower to flower,

Above the owl with perfect sight,
    Who sleeps by day and hunts by night,
Who lives above her neighbor's nest
    (A special place for young to rest)
Beside the cactus tall and grand,
    A haven for creatures in a waterless land.

Some scorpions with stinging tails
    Dance along on unseen trails,
Past rattlesnakes with deadly teeth
    Slip-sliding on the ground beneath
The long-nose bat upon the tower,
    Who spreads the pollen from flower to flower,
Above the owl with perfect sight,
    Who sleeps by day and hunts by night,
Who lives above her neighbor's nest
    (A special place for young to rest)
Beside the cactus tall and grand,
    A haven for creatures in a waterless land.

A den of foxes starts to stir.
    They clean and groom their light brown fur,
While eyeing scorpions with stinging tails
    Who dance along on unseen trails,
Past rattlesnakes with deadly teeth
    Slip-sliding on the ground beneath
The long-nose bat upon the tower,
    Who spreads the pollen from flower to flower,
Above the owl with perfect sight,
    Who sleeps by day and hunts by night,
Who lives above her neighbor's nest
    (A special place for young to rest)
Beside the cactus tall and grand,
    A haven for creatures in a waterless land.

A gila monster with painted back
    Crawls from a hole in search of a snack,
Near foxes who begin to stir
    And clean and groom their light brown fur,
While eyeing scorpions with stinging tails
    Who dance along on unseen trails,
Past rattlesnakes with deadly teeth
    Slip-sliding on the ground beneath

The long-nose bat upon the tower,
    Who spreads the pollen from flower to flower,
Above the owl with perfect sight,
    Who sleeps by day and hunts by night,
Who lives above her neighbor's nest
    (A special place for young to rest)
Beside the cactus tall and grand,
    A haven for creatures in a waterless land.

A world of survivors in a sun-baked land
    Are sheltered and harbored by a cactus grand.
The spiny plant with its weathered face
    Is a noble guard in this busy place.

Exploring the Sahara

By Sarah Canzoneri

Can someone explore the Sahara without going there? Yes. In fact, some of the most exciting discoveries about the Sahara have been made using "explorers" high in the sky—satellites. Thanks to these sky-high explorers, we know more about the history of this amazing desert.

The satellites send down images, or pictures, of Earth. Some are taken by the SIR-A radar system. It can make images that show what is under the ground, below the sand. These images have shown geologists that, in ancient times, there were lakes, mountains, and valleys where the Sahara is now.

So, the Sahara was not always a forbidding desert. Long ago, dinosaurs and giant crocodiles lived there. After the dinosaurs became extinct, giraffes, elephants, hippos, and other animals lived in the Sahara. So did people. They were shepherds and hunters who had small villages and farmed the land. There were forests and grasslands in the Sahara.

Then, about 6,000 years ago, the climate began to change. Within a few centuries, the Sahara became the desert that it is today. Why? Scientists think that conditions in the atmosphere changed so that the Sahara got warmer and drier. As the climate changed, fewer and fewer plants grew there, and the people had to move to places where there was more water.

Excerpt from Appleseed's, April 2002 issue: Exploring the Sahara.
© 2002, Carus Publishing Company, published by Cobblestone Publishing, 30 Grove Street, Suite C, Peterborough, NH 03458. All Rights Reserved. Reprinted by permission of the publisher.

Satellite images help people make other discoveries in the Sahara. With these pictures, archaeologists can find where ancient people had their settlements. Paleontologists—scientists who study fossils to learn about prehistoric life—use satellite images to help them find the best places to search for clues to life millions of years ago.

All Alone in Dinosaur Hall

BY STATON RABIN

The hall of dinosaurs had just closed, and all was quiet. "It's kind of dark here with only the exhibit lights on," my dad said to me. "You sure you won't get scared by yourself?"

"Dad—I'm not a kid anymore!"

"Sorry, Ollie," he said.

My dad works here at our city's natural history museum. He's a paleontologist. That means he studies bones and stuff from animals and plants that lived long ago. Sometimes he works late after the museum has closed and everyone has gone home.

"I've got some paperwork to do," Dad said to me. He looked at his watch. "I'll come back for you at six." Dad disappeared into the darkness, and the sound of his shoes clicking on the marble floors faded away.

I took a look around me. The museum was a very different place at night. The dinosaur hall was dimly lit with creepy blue lights. Even the dinosaur skeletons looked blue. They glowed eerily. And the place was so quiet that I could hear myself breathing.

I walked to the far end of the hall. There was something I hadn't noticed before. A big, white canvas cloth hung from ceiling to floor, hiding an exhibit. The sign said, "Temporarily Closed."

I couldn't resist. I stepped over the rope barrier and walked behind the canvas.

Right in front of me was a new dinosaur! The scientists were putting the bones together, I guess. It looked like a huge model kit that didn't come with instructions. There was a big metal structure all around it for the scientists to climb on. I could tell that the skeleton was nearly complete. That dude must have weighed at least two tons when it was alive!

I sat down on a pile of oval rocks next to the dinosaur to get a better look. (There was no better place to sit.) I got a good look at the skull. The dinosaur had a long, hollow horn on its head. Not like the horn of a rhinoceros. No, this was a long tube from the tip of its snout to the top of its head and beyond. The horn was built right into its face. It looked as if the dinosaur had been in a bad accident with a slide trombone. I wondered if the dinosaur had made noises through that thing.

Then I figured out what kind of dinosaur it was—a *Parasaurolophus* (PAR-uh-sawr-AHL-uh-fus). It was a kind of duckbill dinosaur.

Suddenly I heard a strange crackling sound, like something breaking. The rocks I was sitting on seemed to be moving! I stood up in a hurry.

Creeping Cretaceous Period! I thought. *These aren't rocks—they're eggs! Dinosaur eggs! And they're hatching!*

Don't ask me to explain it. Maybe it had something to do with my sitting on them. I mean, body heat and all—like a chicken sitting on her nest. But dinosaur eggs? Hatching after more than 75 million years?

But hey, it was true! In a moment, a little duckbill poked its head out of one of the eggs. A broken piece of eggshell balanced on its horn. The baby dinosaur shook its little head, and the shell piece went flying. Then the dinosaur squirmed and struggled until it hatched all the way out. Wet from the egg stuff, it wobbled around on its three-toed feet. It looked like a tiny copy of its big mama, except its horn was much shorter.

Just then, the most amazing thing happened. The little dinosaur tooted its tiny horn! It was a soft sound, but very clear. It sounded like a really lousy horn player trying to tune up.

The toot seemed to act like a signal. In a moment, nearly a dozen more of the duckbill eggs started cracking. The baby dinos tumbled out. Some landed on their backs with feet sticking up, and others began walking around, crunching the broken eggshells. They all tooted together, sounding like a bad day at school band practice.

Why am I standing around gaping like an idiot? I thought. *I've gotta get Dad. This could be the most important discovery in the history of paleontology!*

"Listen, you guys," I told the baby duckbills. "Don't—uh—go anywhere. Just keep tooting. I'll be back as soon as I can."

I wanted to pick them up, but I thought it would be too risky—I might hurt them or something. So I ran down the hall, slipping all over the newly mopped floors.

"Hey, Dad!" I yelled when I finally got to his office. "We're both gonna be famous! Tomorrow's newspaper—front page, I guarantee!" I pulled him along by the hand.

"Take it easy, Ollie," he said as I dragged him back into the dinosaur hall. "What's wrong with you? Have you been eating too many candy bars?"

"You just wait and see," I said.

Together we stepped behind the canvas curtain. Gone! Oh, *no!* Every one of them was gone! I just stood there, too stunned to speak. My dad put his hand on my shoulder. "So you've discovered our little secret," he said.

"Secret?"

"Yes. Our pride and joy. We haven't even told the newspapers about it yet," he told me.

"You mean, you *know*?" I said.

"Of course, I know. I'm the head of the department, aren't I? This is our first *Parasaurolophus* exhibit. We're really lucky—these guys are pretty rare. In fact, our museum is the only one with a complete duckbill skeleton in the five-state area!"

"Oh," I said. It was all I could think of to say. I looked around—left and right, up and down. No baby dinosaurs. *Nothing!* Even the dinosaur eggs just looked like a pile of stones.

"Are you all right?" my dad asked. He felt my forehead.

"Sure," I sighed. What was the point of telling him? He'd never believe me. And who could blame him? Even I wouldn't believe me.

My dad shivered. "Come on," he said and put his arm around me. "I'll tell you a secret. I've worked here for 16 years. But at night . . . sometimes, this place gives me the creeps."

"Yeah, Dad?"

"Yeah. I get to imagining, well, all sorts of weird things. Silly, huh?"

"I guess," I said.

The dinosaur hall was quiet except for our breathing. I sneaked one last look around as we walked out together. Nothing. Just imagination, I thought.

My dad locked the gates to the hall. He turned off the main switch to the blue lights. Imagination. Oh, well . . . . "Dad, can we go bass fishing at Rockland Lake next Sunday?" I asked him. "I've been wanting to for the longest . . . "

"Shhh!" he whispered. "Listen."

"Huh?" We stood in the dark, listening. There was a tooting sound coming from somewhere—somewhere very near.

"That's what I love about living in a big city," my dad said. "There's always somebody playing a horn on a street corner. Whew! That guy sure could use a few lessons."

I froze.

"Um, Dad? I think maybe I'd better tell you something . . . . "

Can Hens Give Milk?

BY JOAN BETTY STUCHNER

Shlomo and Rivka lived in the famous town of Chelm, where each person was more foolish than the next. Rivka and Shlomo had five children, twelve hens, one rooster, and not much money.

One day Rivka said, "We have plenty of eggs from our hens, but if we owned a cow, we would also have milk and cheese."

Shlomo thought about what his wife had said. That night he lay in bed and thought about it until he fell asleep. Now, Shlomo was a great dreamer, and this night, sure enough, he had a dream. He dreamed that a cow was eating the fresh, green grass in their tiny field. Then he dreamed that Rivka was milking the cow. He woke with a start and shouted, "That's it!"

The shouting woke Rivka. "What is it, dear husband?"

"Let me ask you a question," Shlomo said excitedly. "Why does a cow give milk?"

"Everyone knows the answer to that," answered Rivka. "A cow gives milk because she eats fresh, green grass."

"Well," said Shlomo with a smile of satisfaction, "doesn't it make sense that if we fed fresh, green grass to our hens, they would not only lay eggs, but also give us milk?"

"Shlomo," said Rivka, "you are a genius."

"Yes," said Shlomo with a blush. "I am."

And they went back to sleep.

"Can Hens Give Milk?" by Joan Betty Stuchner. Reprinted by permission of *Spider* magazine, May 2003, Vol. 10, No. 5, copyright © 2003 by Joan Betty Stuchner.

The next morning Shlomo and Rivka tried to feed fresh, green grass to their hens, but the hens refused this tasty treat. They would eat only corn, as usual.

Shlomo and Rivka couldn't understand. Rivka said, "A cow finds grass irresistible, yet our foolish hens turn up their beaks in disgust. Why is this?"

But Shlomo had already figured out how to solve the problem. "We shall roll the grass into pellets that look like corn. Then they will eat them."

But he was wrong. The hens continued to ignore the grass pellets and ate only the corn. So Shlomo held each hen tightly while Rivka opened its beak and put a pellet inside. The hens clucked angrily, and the grass pellets gave them hiccups.

"That should do the trick," said Rivka.

Before Shlomo and Rivka went to bed that night, Rivka placed a bowl beneath each hen. "In the morning," she said, "we shall surely find that our hens have given us both eggs and milk."

But the next morning when they checked the henhouse, the bowls were empty. Not only was there no milk, but the angry, hiccupping hens had laid no eggs.

"There's only one person who can solve our problem," said Rivka. She sent one of the children to fetch the wise rabbi of Chelm.

When the rabbi arrived, they led him into the henhouse. He examined the hens one by one. He opened their beaks and looked down their throats. He lifted them up and examined their feet. Then he turned them over and checked their stomachs.

"Ah," he said with a wise smile. "I see the problem: these hens are just regular hens. They are not milk hens."

When he saw the disappointment on Shlomo's and Rivka's faces, the rabbi felt sorry for them. "I'll tell you what I'll do," he said. "I have two goats and one lonely rooster at home, but no hens. I will exchange one of my goats for six of your hens. Goats also give good milk. That way you shall have milk, and I shall have eggs."

Shlomo and Rivka cheered up and thanked the rabbi.

The next day they exchanged their hens for his goat. In the future they would have fresh milk and cheese. The remaining six hens were left to eat their corn in peace and began laying eggs once again.

Shlomo looked at the hens eating the corn that helped them lay their eggs. Then he looked thoughtfully at the goat. Goats, he noticed, were so much bigger than hens.

That night Shlomo had a dream. He dreamed that his goat was eating corn. He also dreamed that the goat laid an enormous egg. He woke up suddenly. "Rivka!" he shouted. "I have an idea . . . !"

Snoop, the Search Dog

BY CAROL CARRICK

Snoop is a dog that finds people who are lost. He has helped search for missing children and campers, as well as elderly people who were confused and wandered away from home. Dogs like Snoop are used to search for people all over the world after earthquakes, mud slides, and tornadoes. They can even find people's scents in avalanches and under more than one hundred feet of water. How can they do that?

Did you know that your body gives off a scent that moves in the air like smoke—only it's invisible? This scent floats away from you while you walk, and finally settles on the ground. Snoop tries to pick up the scent that came from a person who is missing, and then goes in that direction. The closer he gets, the stronger the scent will be.

How does he know how to do this? Long before dogs lived with people, they hunted for their own food. Dogs today still have those instincts. Some dogs, like the greyhound, hunt using their eyes, but most dogs use their noses. Snoop's sense of smell is much, much better than ours, which allows him to find missing people faster and more easily than human searchers.

Tracking-and-trailing dogs are given an object to sniff with the lost person's scent on it, such as a glove or shoe.

They hunt only for the person with that scent. But the searchers don't always have something belonging to the lost person. In that case, an air-scenting dog, like Snoop, is given a certain territory to search. He hunts for any person in that area. Since he is not on a leash, he can move more quickly than his handler and cover a large area in less time.

Would your dog make a good search dog? Snoop loves people and wants to please them, and a good search dog isn't skittish in new situations. When a search group arrives, there may be police cars with sirens and radios on, lights, helicopters, other dogs with their handlers, and even newspaper and television reporters—people Snoop doesn't know, some of them very upset because they've lost someone dear to them. During all this noise and confusion, Snoop needs to keep his mind on the job.

Does your dog like to play hide-and-seek? Snoop and his handler train every week. Someone hides in a big field or woods, the kind of place where someone might get lost. Usually the person hides behind a rock or a bush, where she can't be seen. In a city, she might crawl under rubble or go inside a building. When the "lost person" is ready, she radios Snoop's handler, who would be with him when looking for a person who really is lost.

Snoop can hardly wait for his handler to tell him, "Someone's lost. Go find!" so he can begin searching, sniffing the air, hunting for the scent of a human. This is easier when the wind is coming from the direction of the lost person, but a strong wind can scatter the scent and confuse Snoop.

The best time for a dog to search is usually during the early morning or late afternoon or at night, when the temperature is cooler.

When Snoop finds a person, he goes back to tell his handler. (Sometimes he goes back to make sure he hasn't lost his handler too!) Snoop has been trained to tell his handler he has found someone by jumping up and hitting his handler's chest with his front paws. But sometimes Snoop can't find the lost person. In this case, after the search is over, a team member will hide so that Snoop can easily find him and have something to be happy about.

When Snoop's search is successful, though, and he leads his handler and the other searchers to the lost person, everyone makes a big fuss and tells him what a smart and wonderful dog he is. He will also get a "reward"—a tennis ball inside a sock. He loves to have it thrown for him to fetch. But finding the lost person and making his handler happy is Snoop's *real* reward.

Porpoise Savers

BY ELIZABETH SCHLEICHERT

It was a chilly, blustery day on Canada's Grand Manan Island. Owen and Diana, two 14-year-old friends, were excited! They were about to help rescue some harbor porpoises. The porpoises had gotten caught in an offshore fishing pen or weir (WEER).

Harbor porpoises often follow schools of fish called herring, a favorite food. But when the herring swim into a weir, the porpoises sometimes wind up caught there too.

Awhile back, most Grand Manan fishermen would drop a huge net into their weirs to haul up the herring. The porpoises would get netted too—and die. But lately, local fishermen and some scientists have been saving porpoises caught in weirs.

On this day, Owen and Diana first traveled by fishing boat to the weir where the porpoises were trapped. They watched and waited as some of the scientists dived into the water and caught the animals.

By now, Diana and Owen had joined some of the scientists on the research boat. (Owen's dad is a photographer and was taking photos here. That's why the kids got to go on the trip.) The two were just in time to help with the next part of the rescue. The divers had grabbed the porpoises and now were handing them up, one at a time, onto the boat. This wasn't easy! Diana explained, "They were a lot heavier than they looked."

"Porpoise Savers" by Elizabeth Schleichert. Reprinted from the June 2004 issue of *Ranger Rick*® magazine, with the permission of the publisher, the National Wildlife Federation®.

(The kids learned that a single porpoise can weight up to 140 pounds.)

Next the team set to work gathering information on each animal. Scientist Sarah Wong took a blood sample from one of the rescued porpoises. The two kids had an important job too. Owen said, "We had to splash the porpoise with water every few seconds to keep it cool and wet in the open air." This seemed to work. Diana noted, "The animal calmed down a lot." Meanwhile both kids reached over and gently touched the porpoise. It's skin felt like wet rubber," said Diana.

After 10 or 15 minutes of fast-paced work, the scientists were done with the first porpoise. Next step: setting the animal free! (By now the research boat was out beyond the weir.) Owen and Diana watched as two team members plopped the porpoise into the water. Another scientist kept an eye on the last porpoise—its turn was next!

As the rescued porpoises swam off, the two kids cheered. Diana said, "They're such beautiful creatures. It was great helping them." Owen added, "Being that close to the porpoises was awesome!

Since 1991, scientists at the Grand Manan Whale & Seabird Research Station have been busy. Every summer, with the help of local fishermen, they've rescued 20 to 300 porpoises from the island's weirs. And the scientists have learned a lot from their work. For example, they've put satellite tags on some of the porpoises and have been able to track the animal's routes through local waters. All in all, this project has been a success—with the real winners being the porpoises!

Sky Boys: How They Built the Empire State Building

BY DEBORAH HOPKINSON AND JAMES E. RANSOME

It's the end of winter, and your pop's lost his job. So every morning before school you scour the streets for firewood, hunched down in an icy wind.

But look! Here's a pile of wood, free for the taking—all carted off from that old hotel they tore down at Thirty-fourth and Fifth.

Six hundred men are working there—leveling, shoveling, hauling, clearing the rubble away. They're getting ready to make something new, **bold**, SOARING.

A symbol of hope in the darkest of times.

A building, clean and simple and straight as a pencil. And tall, so tall it will scrape the sky.

You drag your pop along to see, and tell him what you've heard on the street.

"Mr. Raskob wants to build the tallest skyscraper in the world," you say, "taller even than Mr. Chrysler's building! They say it'll be done by next May. Think they can build it that fast, Pop?"

"Things are so bad, it seems foolish to even try," he replies. Then he sees your face and adds, "'Course, you never know...."

So let the race begin!

First come rumbling flatbed trucks, bundles of steel on their backs, like a gleaming, endless river surging through the concrete canyons of Manhattan.

This steel is strong and new, only eighty hours old, barely cooled, from the fiery furnaces of Pittsburgh.

Before your eyes a steel forest appears. Two hundred and ten massive columns, lifted by derricks and set onto concrete piers sunk fifty-five feet down to hard-rock bottom. Columns so firm and strong, they can bear the full weight of this giant-to-be: 365,000 tons.

Then it's the sky boys' show. Derrick men hoisting, swinging, easing each beam into place. High overhead they crawl like spiders on steel, spinning their giant web in the sky.

Watch out, sky boys—don't slip in the rain or let the wind whisk you away!

Wouldn't you love to be one of them, the breeze in your face and your muscles as strong as the girder you ride?

Or you could be a water boy, climbing high with your bucket to bring the sky boys a drink. They'd laugh and call out, *"Keep your eyes on the beam, water boy, and don't look down!"*

As each beam is placed, the riveting gang is there to fasten the frame together. Four men work as one.

First man, the Heater, gets the rivet red-hot in the forge and tosses it up quick. (A throw of fifty feet is nothing to him.)

Second man, the Catcher, snares the rivet in his funneled tin can, fishes it out with tongs, and sticks it in the hole.

Third man, the Bucker-up, keeps the rivet nice and steady with his bar.

Fourth man, the Gunman, hammers it into the steel, good and hard.

Toss-catch-steady-pound. Toss-catch-steady-pound. One to two rivets a minute, five hundred rivets a day.

At the same time other workers use six hoists to carry eight-thousand-pound loads of wood and steel right to where they're needed. And on each floor hand-powered railcars on tracks move limestone, pipes, and wires around.

To make work easier, there are temporary elevators, water tanks, and yes, toilets, five lunch stands, and even a restaurant. *No need to leave the job. Get hot beef stew and coffee here, on the unfinished forty-seventh floor!*

In this new, ingenious, assembly-line construction, each man works as fast as he can, knowing that down below a hundred jobless men are ready to take over his spot in a flash. Yet knowing, too, that the quicker he finishes, the sooner he'll be back in line himself, waiting and desperate for work.

From your spot on the sidewalk, you watched the building take shape, bit by bit, piece by piece, like a giant, real-life puzzle, rising four-and-a-half stories each week.

In November the sky boys give a cheer. The skeleton has a skin—all one hundred-and-two stories are done!

And by March the mast on top makes this the tallest building in the world.

Like a general launching an attack, the builder sends in more men—bricklayers, masons, carpenters, electricians, plumbers, all hammering, nailing, wiring, and cutting morning till night, week after week, month after month.

May 1, 1931: opening day. Finished in record time! Sixty thousand tons of steel, ten million bricks, two thousand tons of marble, sixty-five hundred windows, seventy miles of water pipes, eighteen hundred-and-sixty stairs.

One year and forty-five days, seven million man-hours, more than three thousand men—a triumph of speed, safety, and efficiency, and something else, too: beauty.

The ribbon is cut, the crowds swarm in. *"Amazing! Spectacular!" "Now the world can see what New York City's all about!"*

Outside, Pop has a big surprise. "Let's go on up," he suggests with a grin. "I been puttin' our pennies aside."

The crowd sweeps you into the marbled lobby, a tall, grand lady, clothed head to toe in rich, glowing colors. On the center wall a silhouette glitters like a jewel: the Empire State Building, pride of New York City!

To go to the top, it's a buck for adults, two bits for kids. Hop on board for the longest elevator ride of your life. Just swallow if your ears start to hurt.

In no time you're there, but even on tiptoe you can't see a thing. Then *whoosh!* You're up on Pop's back.

"Gee whiz!" you shout. "We're on top of the world."

Pop shakes his head, disbelieving. "If we can do this, we can do anything," he says.

Itching to see it all, you jump down and race round the deck. North and south and east and west, all Manhattan lies at your feet.

"Say, Pop," you call, "do you think there's a kid just like me way down there, looking at us up here?"

After a while the sun slips away; tiny lights and stars flicker on. Bright threads of taxis lace the darkness below; the great city shimmers and hums.

All around, folks are starting to leave. You beg, "Please, Pop, a few minutes more?"

But it's time. So, with one last look, you head down to earth.

On the long walk home you're fuzzy with sleep, holding tight to your father's rough hand.

But then at the corner you turn and stop short in surprise.

"Look, Pop, we can still see it from here!"

Oh, how it lights up the night.

Taking Flight
The Story of the Wright Brothers

WRITTEN BY STEPHEN KRENSKY

The cloth-covered kite looked like a very strange bird. It rose and fell on the wind, turning with each new breeze. But this was not a small bird. It had two five-foot wings, one set above the other.

From the ground below, a balding thirty-two-year-old man controlled the glider like an upside-down puppet. His name was Wilbur Wright.

Cords ran from the glider's wings to crossed sticks in Wilbur's hands. When he pulled the sticks down to the left, the glider's left wing tip twisted—and the glider curved to the left. If he pulled the sticks down to the right the right wing tip twisted—and the glider curved to the right.

Wilbur and his brother Orville had built the glider in nearby Dayton, Ohio. There they had a shop where they built and sold bicycles. They liked to use their hands to tinker with a printing press or build a new porch for the house they shared with their father and sister.

The Wrights had been interested in flying objects for a long time. In 1878, when Wilbur was eleven and Orville just seven, their father had given them a surprise. "Father brought home to us a small toy actuated by a rubber spring." Orville later wrote, "which would lift itself into the air." This little helicopter—made of bamboo, paper, and cork—excited both boys. Soon they were building their own small flying machines.

The Wrights carried into adulthood their dream of flying, but such dreams were not new. The subject of flight had been popular since ancient times. In one Greek myth, the architect Daedelus made two sets of wings from feathers and wax. He and his son, Icarus, used them to fly across the sea. The wings worked until Icarus flew too close to the sun. When the sun's heat melted the wax, Icarus fell into the sea.

Fortunately, Orville and Wilbur weren't working with wax and feathers, but with a glider made of wood. When Wilbur met Orville after testing the kite, he told his brother that they were on the right track. It was possible to control a glider's flight by twisting or warping its wings.

This kind of control was important. The Wrights worried, after all, about what would happen after the aircraft was aloft. They had no interest in hot-air balloons, which only drifted on the wind. The Wrights wanted to steer their own way through the air.

Orville was pleased by Wilbur's report, but not surprised. He and Wilbur had thought long and hard before building the glider, as they did about almost everything. They worked together, ate together, and sometimes finished each other's sentences. Wilbur was quieter than Orville—who had a mustache and wore fancier clothes—but the two brothers were closer than twins.

They had already read the few books about flying machines they could find. They also had begun to study birds in flight. The wing-warping was a test of what they had learned so far.

Wilbur wrote to his father, who was away from home, that he was exploring the subject ". . . for pleasure rather than profit." That was wise, because the birds made flying look far easier than it really was.

Fleece, Fiber, Yarn, Sweater

BY MAUREEN ASH

"I like the brown one," said Leslie.

"I like the gray one," said Brie. The girls stood by the fence and watched the two llamas. The llamas watched them right back.

A lady came out of the barn. "Hi," she said cheerfully. "Are you my new neighbors?"

"We just moved in over thee," Leslie pointed across the road at their new house. "I'm Leslie and she's Brie."

"Pleased to meet you," said the lady. "I'm Stacy, and those handsome boys are Cal and Sterling, my llamas."

Cal, the brown one, and Sterling, the gray one, walked over to stand near Stacy. They looked at the girls with their big brown eyes and blinked.

"They have long eyelashes," said Brie.

"And long ears and long necks," added Leslie.

"And long coats," Stacy laughed. "But I'll soon take care of that. After I brush them this morning, I'm going to shear them."

"You mean cut off their fur?" Leslie asked.

"On llamas we usually call it hair or fiber," Stacy explained as she brushed Sterling. "Cal and Sterling get a haircut once a year, and today is the big day. Would you like to watch?"

"Yes!" said the girls. It was fun to see the thick blanket of fiber fall to the ground as Stacy ran the clippers back and forth across first Sterling and then Cal. The llamas didn't seem to mind one bit, but they looked funny without their fleeces.

"Now they're just in their long underwear and hats," said Leslie.

"I think they're glad about that because it's getting hot," said Brie. "What will you do with all this fiber, Stacy?"

"Well," said Stacy. "You're right. One reason I shear the boys is because they'd be too hot all summer in that thick, warm fleece. But I don't have a fleece for when it gets cold, so I'm going to use some of theirs to make a sweater."

"Wow!" said Brie. "Can we watch that too?"

Stacy laughed. "It takes quite a while, Brie. But if you girls come over tomorrow, you can help me get started."

The next day Stacy showed Leslie and Brie how to pick the sticks and dirt out of the llama fiber and sort it by color. Cal's fiber was dirtier than Sterling's. "He's just messy," Stay said. "Llamas like to roll in the dirt to cool off and scratch their back, but I think Cal *tries* to get dirty!"

Even after being picked over, the fiber turned the water in the tub brown with dirt when Stacy began washing it. The girls helped Stacy dump the dirty water and gently wash the fiber over and over until the water stayed clean. Then they spread the clean fiber to dry on a net stretched in Stacy's workroom.

Walking home past the llama pasture, the girls saw Cal rolling in the dirt. Sterling was taking a nap in the grass. "Oh, Cal," Brie giggled, "aren't you brown enough already?"

When the girls returned a few days later, Stacy showed them her two carding paddles. Each paddle had rows of small, sharp wires sticking out of one side. Stacy took a bit of fiber, placed it on one paddle, and then put the other paddle on top of that and pulled them apart. "See how carding the fiber straightens it?" she asked. "That makes it easier to spin into yarn."

Brie couldn't wait to try it, but pulling the paddles apart was hard. She could barely move them. "That's OK," said Stacy, "You can use the drum carder."

Stacy showed the girls how to turn the crank to make the big and the little drums on the drum carder spin. The drums had wires sticking out of them, just like the carding paddles. Stacy fed some fiber under the smaller drum, and as the drums turned around and around, the wires combed and straightened the fiber.

Turning the drum carder was fun. Soon they had a pile of combed fibers and it was time to go home. "When you come back, I'll show you how to spin," Stacy promised.

The spinning wheel worked by twisting the loose fibers together into a single strong strand and winding it on a spool. The girls spent all morning learning to guide the fluffy fibers and pedal the spinning wheel. "I'm getting dizzy!" exclaimed Leslie. But by lunchtime they had a spool full of yarn.

Week after week the girls helped Stacy spin. Some days they took a break and she taught them to knit. But mostly they spun. It was fall and almost time for school to start when Stacy finally said, "I need to wash the yarn one more time, but I think we have enough for three sweaters."

Every day after school, Brie and Leslie helped Stacy do chores. They loved feeding and talking to Cal and Sterling, who learned to wait at the gate to see the girls get off the bus. And when the chores were done, the girls knit.

Slowly they finished the backs of their sweaters. They finished the fronts. At last, they finished the arms, and Stacy helped them stitch the pieces together.

The next Saturday was the first snowy day of the winter, and that day the girls wore their sweaters for the first time. They ran to show Stacy, who was heading out to the barn.

"Look!" said Brie and Leslie.

"Look!" said Stacy, pointing to Cal and Sterling, whose warm, soft coats were getting thick again. The llamas stood at the gate, watching the girls.

Leslie laughed. "You look like Sterling!" she told Brie.

"And you look like Cal!" Brie answered. "All this time we've been working on our sweaters, they've been growing their own."

The llamas just blinked as snow fell on them all.

Water Works

BY ELIZABETH CARNEY

On the surface, Ryan Hreljac (hurl-**jack**) seems like a typical 15-year-old. He plays ice hockey, football, and basketball. He loves computer games and isn't crazy about chores. "I hate vacuuming the most!" Ryan says.

But this teen from Kemptville, Canada, has already accomplished extraordinary things. Ryan and his organization, the Ryan's Well Foundation, have built 245 wells that provide clean water to nearly 400,000 people in 11 countries, mostly in Africa. "I spend half my time helping the world with clean water projects and the other half being a teenager," Ryan says.

How did Ryan build so many wells at such a young age? He has actually been doing this for nine years! When Ryan was 6, his first-grade teacher told his class that millions of people around the world don't have safe drinking water and decent sanitation services. As a result, many people, including children, become sick and sometimes die.

That's all Ryan needed to hear. He did chores to earn $70 toward building a well in Africa. Then came disappointing news. A charity called WaterCan told Ryan that a well would cost at least $2,000. "That's OK," he said. "I'll just do more chores."

With the help of his parents, his community, and other charity organizations, Ryan's first well was built in Uganda in 1999. Ryan started with $70; he has now raised more than $1.5 million! He has traveled to Africa many times to see the wells built in his name. While there, he has made many friends, including one whom he now calls brother.

People worldwide suffer from a lack of clean water. "Many people don't know that over a billion people in the world struggle to have this basic necessity of life," Ryan explains.

The International Committee of the Red Cross says a person needs at least four to five gallons of water a day for drinking, cooking, bathing, and sanitation. Some people struggle to live on as few as three gallons a day, says Ryan's Well Foundation. On the other hand, people in the U. S. use more water than people do anywhere else in the world—a range of 100 to 176 gallons a day per person.

Why do some people struggle to get clean water? War, violence, and lack of money are three big reasons that some governments can't provide the building blocks for clean water—like pipes, sewers, and water treatment plants—for all their citizens. So, sometimes people only have access to water that is dirty, smelly, and contaminated.

While Ryan is tackling a serious worldwide issue, he's quick to point out how others have helped him. "I always believed that I could make a difference and I still do," Ryan says. "But I didn't do it alone. I started by asking my parents for guidance."

The Ryan's Well Foundation also works with organizations like Rotary International and Uganda's Ruhinda Women's Group. "They help us figure out which projects make the most sense," Ryan says.

What's Ryan's advise for kids who want to make a difference? "Kids should find something that they really care about. Then think about what small steps they can take to do something about it," he says.

Ryan could always use some help: "There's still so much to do, but that's no reason to stop."

Down Girl and Sit Save the Day

BY LUCY NOLAN

Down Girl and her neighbor, Sit, are two very busy dogs. They work together to keep the world safe from thieving squirrels and birds. Down Girl's master, Rruff, can be forgetful at times, but Down Girl loves him with all her heart. She would do anything to be helpful.

In the following story, Down Girl and Sit work together to find their "lost" masters and lead them safely home.

It's not easy being a dog. There are too many things to remember.

For instance, we have to remember that new shoes are not playthings. Bumblebees are not playthings either.

If we didn't have such large brains, we might become as forgetful as our masters.

The other day Rruff forgot to eat breakfast. I couldn't believe it. Rruff never starts the day without toast or a doughnut.

At least he put my coffee where I could reach it.

"Down, girl!"

"Rruff!" I love that man.

We met Sit and her master for our walk. When the walk was over, all four of us ended up in my backyard. Did Sit's master forget where they really lived?

Reprinted from *Down Girl and Sit: Smarter than Squirrels* by Lucy Nolan with permission of Marshall Cavendish Corp.

Oh, well. Sit and I didn't say anything. We knew something our masters did not know. As soon as our leashes were off, we would play together in my yard. We ran around, chasing each other, while our masters smiled.

But wait! Our masters had somehow gotten out of the fence when we weren't looking. They were riding off on bicycles. Here's the worst part. They forgot us!

I jumped against the gate. I barked and barked. Suddenly the gate swung open. I actually opened the gate! I thought I was brilliant. Sit thought the gate was unlocked to begin with.

It didn't matter. Sit and I were free. We could go after our masters!

I turned to Sit. "Should we walk or take the car?"

Ha! I am just too funny!

We saw which way our masters went. We ran in that direction. We put our noses to the ground and followed their trail. After three blocks, we began to lose the scent.

"It's time to quit following our noses and start following our brains," I said.

Where could our masters possibly be?

"Perhaps they stopped to roll in that leaf pile," Sit said. That was an excellent suggestion!

Sit and I trotted over to it. Our masters weren't anywhere in sight. That didn't mean they weren't hiding down deep in that pile.

Sit and I sniffed it. We didn't smell Rruff. We could tell that a poodle, a collie and two cocker spaniels had been there. Quite frankly, the leaf pile stunk. We jumped right in.

If our masters had passed up this much fun, they must have gone somewhere even better. Where could that be?

"Perhaps they went to swim in the creek," I said.

That was another good idea!

Sit and I splashed all through the creek. When we climbed out, we were covered with green pond scum.

"Ha!" I told Sit. "You look like a salad!"

We laughed and crept along, pretending to be salads. Then we remembered salads don't creep. They don't do anything at all. They just sit there. That kind of took the fun out of it.

Where else could our masters be? We were running out of places to look. It was time to think about this more deeply.

"It we weren't at home, where would we be?" I asked.

Finally the obvious answer hit us.

"We'd go to the park to chase squirrels!" we both shouted.

This was our best idea yet.

When we got to the park, our masters weren't there. We chased squirrels anyway. We didn't even do it to save the world. We did it just for fun.

After a while, Sit and I began to wonder if we would ever see our masters again. We were feeling very sad.

All of a sudden I caught the whiff of something familiar in the air. I quivered all over with excitement. I couldn't believe what my nose was telling me.

"Is it Rruff?" Sit asked.

"No!" I said. "It's a doughnut!"

Sit and I followed the scent. We went up one street and down another. Then we found the most amazing place. People were sitting and eating at tables outside. Doughnuts were everywhere.

Quite frankly, I'm surprised we were the only dogs there.

Then I saw Rruff. He was eating with Sit's master. We wagged our tails and ran to them.

"Down, girl!"

"Sit!"

Our masters did not seem happy to see us. We tried to leave, but they didn't want us to. I wish they'd learn to make up their minds.

Our masters invited us to lie down next to them. In fact, they insisted on it.

I was being good. I really was. Then I saw a man at the table next to us. He had a bag of doughnuts.

I did the only thing I could do. I inched my way over to him and begged. I did this in a very cool way, of course. When you beg in a cool way, it is not called begging. It is called staring.

The man pulled out a newspaper. He pushed the bag of doughnuts to the edge of the table.

Why, thank you! What a generous man.

"Down, girl!"

I looked up. Rruff was heading towards me. What? Was it time to go already?

Okay, I could finish my doughnuts on the way.

I ran between the tables. Rruff ran after me. The man did too. It was so much fun, I did it again. So did Rruff. Everywhere I ran, Rruff was right behind me. Why was he following me everywhere? That's when I figured it out. He must have forgotten how to get home by himself.

Thank goodness Sit and I knew the way.

We ran through the neighborhood. Our masters stuck close behind us on their bicycles. They were shouting the whole way. Were they afraid we would leave them behind?

It was hard to run with the doughnuts. I knew Rruff was depending on me to get him home. I kept going. I didn't even stop to chase squirrels in the park.

Okay, maybe I chased one or two.

When we got home, I ran through the open gate. I sat in the backyard to wait.

Rruff finally rolled up, huffing and puffing. Perhaps he should cut down on the doughnuts.

Sit and I ate the whole bag ourselves.

Then I ran to greet Rruff. He leaned against the house, panting. I kissed him.

"Down, girl!"

That's what I love about Rruff. He is very forgetful, but in the end he always remembers what's important. He remembers me. He remembers that I am his best friend in the world.

And even though he gets out of the fence from time to time, he always remembers to come home.

A Ducky Day

BY MARGARET FLING

It was a perfect morning—the clean, rain-washed shades of green were all around me as I plucked wilted petunia blossoms off the plants on the front deck. A weak squeak from the large flowerpot in the far corner behind me joined the sounds of late spring.

This surprise had arrived three weeks earlier. We had returned home from vacation in mid-April and discovered that the flowers in this particular pot had been eaten. In their place lay three duck eggs in a dirt nest. Each day after that, the mallard hen flew over our fence to lay another tan egg until eight filled the nest. Our deck made the eggs safe from foxes, raccoons, and neighbors' cats.

On the ninth day the duck settled down to hatch her babies. She sat on her nest nearly twenty-four hours a day, drinking and eating very little. She ate only the stems and flowers from the nearest pots and the cereal, bread crusts, and water we set out for her. She followed us closely with her eyes and scrunched down in her nest whenever we watered the flowers or cooked on the grill. A weekend guest who didn't know about our "other guest" went out on the deck one morning to read the newspaper. Thinking the duck was a decoration, she was startled to see Mama duck get up, stretch, and shift position.

We checked the duck each day and were as anxious as she was for the ducklings to hatch. Finally, after twenty-eight days, the moment had come. Although the eggs had been laid over a period of nine days, eight fuzzy, yellow-and-brown ducklings cracked through their shells within only a couple hours of each other.

Then Mama duck shook out her feathers, balanced herself on the rim of her flowerpot nest as if to say, "Well, that's done," and leaped onto the deck floor. Her brood of eight immediately scrambled up each others' backs to get up to the pot's rim and then fell with soft plops to the floor two feet below. With no brother's or sister's back left to climb up on, the last baby had the most difficult time, but Mama stood below and waited patiently. When at last surrounded by all eight peeping ducklings, she started teaching them how to survive by taking them to the water dish and showing them how to drink.

Soon, though, she realized she had a big problem: How could she get her babies off the enclosed deck? She waddled back and forth, searching for an opening. She looked at the top railing but decided it was too high for them, since they couldn't fly yet. At first we had planned to put the ducklings in a box and take them to the pond, but Mama duck got upset when we tried to pick the babies up. Finally we had an idea: Would she come through the house if we opened the doors to both the front and back decks, since the back deck had openings that Mama and the babies could easily slip through?

We stood near the door trying to coax Mama into entering the room, but that only sent her farther away.

Next we tried to herd the ducklings through the door by getting behind them and flapping our arms. They ran to a far corner of the deck in panic. Then I wondered if she thought the babies couldn't make it over the high threshold, so we found some wood in the garage and set up a ramp. Then we stood back and quietly waited inside the house.

Mama checked out the ramp—she walked up, looked in the door, and went back down. Then she gathered up the crew and walked up again, but only two ducklings followed her. She quacked at them and went out again.

The next try brought four into the house. She turned around and quacked out more orders that sounded something like: "Get up here! Now!" In a flash, all eight were up the ramp and in the house. She marched straight past the table, the hall stairs, through the living room, and out onto the back deck, followed by her eight babies in a single-file line.

Without looking back, she jumped off the open deck to the ground below. The little ones tumbled over each other, falling off the deck as if running from a fire. They ran to catch up, because Mama didn't wait or even turn around. She headed straight through the woods for the pond, with her eight adorable balls of fluff hurriedly waddling after her.

The Secret Project

BY JOAN STEVENSON

Annie loved watching birds from the family-room window. She eagerly waited for them to come and start building their nests in the spring.

One Saturday morning Annie sat lacing her sneakers. Beside her, Great-Aunt Lizzie was knitting a lovely, colorful afghan. Annie was daydreaming about the birds that would soon come to the tree outside the window. Suddenly one of her purple shoelaces snapped off in her fingers.

"Oh, these are my favorite laces," she cried.

As Annie was about to toss the broken lace into a wastebasket, she noticed Great-Aunt Lizzie's beautiful skeins of yarn. She looked again at her pieces of purple shoelace. An idea popped into her head.

"Aunt Lizzie, can you spare a few pieces of yarn?" she asked.

"Of course, honey," Great-Aunt Lizzie said. "I'll snip you some of each color."

"Thank you," said Annie. Then she hurried to find her mother.

"Mommy, do we have any of those net bags that hold onions?" she asked.

"Yes. Why?" Mommy asked.

"I need one for a secret project," Annie said. "Would it be O.K. if I take one?"

"Sure," Mommy said. "Look in the kitchen cupboard."

Annie placed her shoelace pieces and strands of yarn in the mesh bag. Then she pulled at the laces and yarn so they dangled out the holes.

Her father was doing laundry, and Annie poked her head in the doorway.

"Daddy, do you have some fluffy lint I can have?" she asked.

"Lint?" Daddy asked. "Why in the world would you want lint?"

"It's a secret project," Annie said.

Daddy opened the dryer door and scooped out a handful of soft, clean lint from the filter. "Fresh from the last load of towels," he said.

"Great! Thanks, Daddy," Annie said, stuffing the lint into the onion bag.

Big sister Kaitlin was cutting out a dress pattern on the dining room table. "Could I have some scraps of cloth?" Annie asked.

"No problem," Kaitlin said.

Annie tore the cloth scraps into long, thin strips and stuffed them into the onion bag.

Next, Annie ran to the pile of firewood on the back porch. She searched through the pile until she found several bits of bark and some gray, scraggly moss.

"Perfect," she exclaimed. Then she stuffed the bark and moss into the onion bag.

Annie found a coat hanger in her closet. She attached the onion bag to it, and her secret project was finished.

Swinging the onion bag, she danced through the house. "Kaitlin! Daddy! Mommy! Aunt Lizzie!" she called. "Come and see my secret project." Annie pulled her father by the hand. "Now I need someone very tall," she said, leading Daddy into the backyard. Everyone followed.

Annie pointed to the pine tree just outside the family-room window.

"Please lift me up so I can reach that branch, Daddy," she said.

Daddy lifted Annie high over his head, and she slipped the hanger around the branch. The onion bag swayed in the breeze. Pieces of bright fabric, yarn, shoelace, and moss poked out every which way through the holes in the net.

"This year, when we watch the birds build nests for their families," Annie said, "we can watch them build with things from *our* family."

Isabel and the Shy Giant

BY HARRIET SCOTT CHESSMAN

One morning Mama said, "I need to sail to Aunt Rose's house for seven days to help with her new baby."

"But I'll miss you," said Isabel.

"I'll miss you, too," said Mama.

"What if giants come to our island and sit in our house and squash our garden?" asked Isabel.

"Oh my, Isabel, I don't think giants will come," said Mama. "And Grandma will be here with you."

"You never know about giants," said Isabel.

"Well, if you see one, I hope you'll tell me all about it," said Mama.

"I'll write about it," said Isabel, "and make pictures too."

Mama gave Isabel seven hugs—one for each day she would be away. Isabel gave Mama seven kisses. Soon Mama was out of sight.

Isabel sewed pieces of paper together to make a book. She wrote in it each day, and Grandma helped with the spelling. And here it is:

MONDAY

Today Mama went on a boat to Aunt Rose's house.

I hope a giant does not come—especially one with big feet and a hairy nose.

Grandma says she thinks I can handle any giant.

TUESDAY

I went fishing in the cove with Grandma. We ate sandwiches in the boat. My sandwich got wet.

I missed Mama.

I saw a giant peeking at us from behind a rock. His hair looked silly standing straight up on his head.

I told Grandma about the giant, and she thought maybe he was hungry. I held out an apple, but he disappeared. He is a shy giant.

WEDNESDAY

I went to the beach to find shells. I'm saving the best ones for Mama: a conch and a lady's finger.

I saw the giant's footprints in the sand. Maybe he was looking for shells too.

I think he lives on an island just for giants. His mama must wonder where he goes each day.

THURSDAY

Today I had a cold. Grandma put me to bed and gave me lemonade. The giant came to visit. He was very polite. He said, "Hello. My name is Hodge."

I said, "Hello. My name is Isabel."

Hodge was too big to come in, so he sat outside my window. I showed him how to play go fish, and then he showed me how to balance shells on my nose.

FRIDAY

My cold was better. Grandma let me play outside. Hodge came, and we made a circus for Grandma.

I climbed up on Hodge's shoulders and jumped into his hands. He was careful not to step on the garden. He juggled watermelons, and I juggled lemons. I was a clown and tumbled under Hodge's legs.

Grandma said it was the best circus she ever saw.

SATURDAY

Today we had a big adventure. Hodge got lost at sea, and I had to go and rescue him. I sailed for miles and miles until I found him crying on an island.

He was glad to see me. He held on to my boat, and I pulled him all the way home.

SUNDAY

I went to the dock with Hodge to watch the fishermen.

I told Hodge that Mama was coming home tomorrow. He said his mama must be missing him and that he should go home too.

I gave him seven hugs and told him to come back soon.

On Monday morning Mama came up the walk. Isabel jumped into her arms.

"I'm glad you're home," said Isabel.

"I'm glad too," said Mama.

"I met a giant," said Isabel.

"Oh my," said Mama.

"You can read all about him," said Isabel, and she gave Mama the book.

"A book for me?" said Mama. "By my Isabel! Give me a hug, and let's read it together."

And they did.

Anna Moves In

BY NANCY ZIMMERER

Toby lived in a big, yellow house. Anna's family had just moved into the big, white house next-door.

"Why doesn't Anna talk?" Toby asked his mommy.

"She talks with her hands," Toby's mommy said. "She uses sign language because she can't hear. She's deaf."

Toby looked down at his own hands. How can hands talk? he wondered.

One day, Anna's mother came to visit. "Toby," she said, "would you like to play with Anna?"

Toby looked out the window. Anna was sitting on the grass watching Toby's cat, Patches, clean his fur.

"But I don't know how to make my hands talk," Toby said.

Anna's mother smiled. "That's O.K., Toby. Anna is very good at guessing what you say by watching your lips. Just be sure she is looking at you when you talk to her."

Toby looked out the window again.

"Would you like to learn how to make your hands say cat before you go outside?" Anna's mother asked.

Toby nodded. "Yes, please."

Anna's mother reached up and pulled two pretend whiskers on her face.

Toby laughed.

She did it again. "Cat," she said. "I just signed the word cat. Now you try."

Toby tried and soon he was pulling pretend whiskers, too. He ran to the mirror to see. "Cat," he said as he made the whiskers sign. "Meow!" he said as he made the sign again. He turned back to Anna's mother. "Thank you," he said. "Now I'm going to show Anna!"

When Toby ran outside, Anna had her back to him. She didn't turn around until he tapped her on the shoulder. Then she waved hello.

Toby waved back. He made the whiskers sign.

"Cat," Toby said, pointing to the black and white kitty.

Anna smiled so big that her eyes almost disappeared.

"Cat!" she said with her lips. She pulled pretend whiskers on her face, too.

Soon Toby was showing Anna all his favorite play spots.

When Toby showed her his climbing tree, Anna bent her arm with her fingers in the air.

"Tree," Toby said as he tried to imitate Anna.

Anna smiled and pointed to a squirrel. She held her fingers in front of her and tapped them together. "Squirrel," she said with her lips. When Toby tried, he pretended to chew like a squirrel. Anna giggled and started climbing the tree. Toby followed her.

"Toby, it's time for lunch," his mother called.

"O.K.! We're coming," Toby answered.

He quickly climbed down the tree, but Anna didn't come. Oh no! How could he tell her about lunch?

Suddenly, Toby had an idea. He pretended to eat an imaginary bowl of his favorite food, spaghetti! Then he pointed to the house.

Anna watched for a moment. Then she made her fingers touch her thumb and lifted them to her mouth. She stared to chew.

"Eat!" Toby said. "That must be the sign for eat."

Anna nodded, climbed out of the tree, and turned to Toby. She held up her pointer fingers and slowly hooked them. Then she hooked them the other way and pointed to Toby.

"Friend," she mouthed.

Toby copied her hands and nodded. "Friends!" he agreed and then he smiled.

Anna smiled back, and together they ran to the house.

The Hippopotamus and a Monkey's Heart

A FOLK TALE FROM CAMEROON
ADAPTED BY TOLOLWA M. MOLLEL

A hippopotamus offered a ride to a little monkey who lived in a tree by a big river. It was a nice morning, bright and clear, with a breeze gently rippling the water. Perched on the hippopotamus, the monkey closed his eyes in contentment, enjoying his first-ever water voyage.

In the middle of the river, the hippopotamus, with much sadness, said to the monkey, "Our chief is ill and dying, and our medicine man says that only a monkey's heart can cure him. So, if you hold on tight, I'll make a quick dip down to the under-river, and we shall just be in time to save him."

The little monkey looked into the bottomless river and at the frightening expanse of water around him. In the distance the riverbanks gleamed in the early sunlight, and swans splashed gaily about.

It's too beautiful a morning to get into this much trouble, thought the little monkey, and he replied most graciously to the hippopotamus.

"Oh, how you flatter me! I never could have imagined that a monkey as humble and worthless as I would be called upon to save as precious a life as that of your most noble chief! If I had known of the honor awaiting me,

The Hippopotamus and a Monkey's Heart adapted by Tololwa M. Mollel. Originally appeared in *Spider* magazine. Reprinted by Permission of the author.

I would have come prepared. As it is, I was so excited at the thought of a ride across the river that I swung down without my heart! You might not know it, but we monkeys keep our hearts locked away and only wear them on important occasions."

"That's all right," said the hippopotamus with perfect understanding. "I'll take you back and wait while you fetch it."

When they reached the shore, the little monkey quickly dashed up a tree and looked down at the patient bulk of the hippopotamus. "Whew! That was close!" he muttered and related what had happened (or almost happened) to the other monkeys. They roared with laughter at the little monkey's quick thinking and the daftness of the hippopotamus.

And to this day, the monkeys still remember the incident and chatter excitedly about it.

As for the hippopotamus, he waited and waited and waited; occasionally he comes on land to see what on earth is taking the little monkey so long.

Wiley and the Hairy Man

ADAPTED FROM AN AMERICAN FOLK TALE
BY MOLLY GARRETT BANG

A long time ago, a boy named Wiley lived with his mother near a swamp in Mississippi. One day Wiley needed some bamboo to make poles for a hen roost. The only place to get bamboo was in the swamp, but that was where the Hairy Man lived. And the Hairy Man would get you if you didn't watch out.

"I'll take the hound dogs with me," Wiley said to his mother. "The Hairy Man can't stand hound dogs."

But Wiley's mother shook her head. "Leave your dogs tied up at home," she said. "You can't be scared of the Hairy Man forever. A time comes when you have to stand up to him." And Mother told Wiley just what to do if he saw the Hairy Man.

Well, as soon as Wiley got to the swamp, he did see the Hairy Man coming at him through the trees. He sure was ugly. He had hair all over, his eyes were burning like coals, and his teeth were big and sharp. The Hairy Man was swinging a sack, and he was grinning because he knew in a minute he would have Wiley inside it.

Wiley wanted to run away, but he stayed put and said, "Hello, Hairy Man. I hear you can change yourself into something else."

"I reckon I can," said the Hairy Man.

"I bet you can't change yourself into a giraffe," said Wiley.

"Sure I can," the Hairy Man said. "That's no trouble at all." The Hairy Man twisted around, and he changed himself into a giraffe.

So Wiley said, "Everybody can change into something big. I bet you can't change yourself into a little possum."

The giraffe twisted around and changed itself into a little possum. In a wink, Wiley grabbed the possum and threw it into the Hairy Man's sack. He tied the sack as tight as he could, and threw it into the Tombigbee River. Then Wiley started back home through the swamp, feeling strong and happy.

But he hadn't gone far, when there was the Hairy Man again, coming at Wiley. He looked uglier and meaner than ever. Wiley climbed right up the nearest tree.

"How did you get out?" he called down.

"I changed myself into the wind," said the Hairy Man, "and I blew my way out. Now I'm going to wait right down here. Sooner or later, you'll get hungry and you'll have to come down."

Wiley studied the situation. He thought about the Hairy Man waiting below, and he thought with longing about his hound dogs tied up at home.

After a while Wiley said, "Hairy Man, you did some pretty good tricks. But I bet you can't make things disappear."

The Hairy Man said, "Ha! That's what I'm best at. Look at your shirt, Wiley." Wiley looked down. His shirt was gone!

"Oh, that was just a plain old shirt," he said. "But this rope around my pants is magic. My mother pulled it from the air one day. I bet you can't make this rope disappear."

The Hairy Man said, "I can make all the rope in this county disappear."

"Bet you can't," said Wiley.

The Hairy Man threw out his chest, opened his wide mouth, and hollered loud, "All the rope in this county, DISAPPEAR!"

The rope around Wiley's pants was gone. He held his pants up with one hand, and held on to the tree with the other; and he hollered loud, "HERE dogs!" The dogs came running and the Hairy Man fled.

Whistling, Wiley made his way through the forest, and never again did he fear the Hairy Man or his magic.

Teddy's Bear

By Janeen R. Adil

Theodore "Teddy" Roosevelt, America's twenty-sixth president, was famous for accomplishing many important things while he was in office. Something he didn't do, however, made him just as famous. And because of it, one of the best-loved toys ever created was named after him.

In November 1902, President Roosevelt traveled south to settle a boundary dispute between Mississippi and Louisiana. While he was there, he took some time off to go bear hunting. Several reporters and a well-known newspaper artist named Clifford Berryman joined the president's hunting trip.

The hunters didn't have much luck. Finally, on the last day of the hunt, the president spotted a bear. As he carefully aimed his rifle, the animal turned around. It was only a cub! Teddy Roosevelt loved to hunt, but he refused to shoot this frightened little bear.

Clifford Berryman thought this was a wonderful opportunity for a drawing. He sketched a cartoon of President Roosevelt turning his back on the cub, unwilling to shoot the small creature. Soon Berryman's black-and-white drawing was appearing in newspapers all over the country. People everywhere liked the cartoon and thought it showed the president to be a kind-hearted man.

"Teddy's Bear" by Janeen R. Adil. Reprinted by permission of *Spider* magazine, May 1998, Vol. 5, No. 5, copyright © 1998 by Janeen R. Adil.

One of those who saw and enjoyed the drawing was Morris Michtom, a candy store owner in Brooklyn, New York. He and his wife, Rose, knew how to make stuffed toys, and the cartoon gave them an idea. The Michtoms found some brown plush fabric and cut out pieces for a bear with movable arms and legs. Then they sewed and stuffed the bear and added buttons for its eyes.

The Michtoms placed the new toy bear, a copy of Berryman's cartoon, and a sign that read "Teddy's Bear" in the front window of their store. The bear sold quickly, and so did the next few that the Michtoms made. When Morris saw how popular the bears were, he knew he would need the president's permission to continue using his name.

Morris wrote a letter to the White House and received a handwritten reply from Theodore Roosevelt himself. "I don't think my name is likely to be worth much in the bear business," the president wrote, "but you are welcome to use it." So the Michtoms went to work, making one teddy bear after another.

Since Rose and Morris made the bears themselves and still had a candy store to manage, they produced the bears slowly at first. Eventually they closed the candy store, and the Michtom family business became the Ideal Toy Company, one of America's biggest toymakers. Soon other companies in the United States and Europe were producing bears of all shapes, sizes, and prices. Some of the most beautiful stuffed bears were made in Germany by Margarete Steiff and her workers.

In just a few years, teddy bears had become extremely popular.

Other items related to the stuffed bears were sold too. Not only could one buy clothing for a teddy bear, but there were also bear puzzles, bear books, bear games, bear banks—all sort of toys and amusements! Teddy bears had become as important to children as blocks, dolls, and balls had already been for generations.

Today teddy bears remain a favorite of boys and girls everywhere. Many adults love to collect and display them too. Hundreds of millions of teddy bears have been produced since Teddy Roosevelt's hunting trip so many years ago. Who could have guessed that the story of an unlucky president and a frightened bear cub would have such a happy ending?

The Experiment

BY MARY ANN JOST

"Try not to make too much noise," Dad said as he headed toward his office. "I have a lot of work to do this afternoon. And don't make a mess," he added. "Grandma's coming, remember?"

Abby and her little brother Joey sat down in the middle of the kitchen floor to think of something to do.

"I have an idea," Abby said. "Let's be scientists. Scientists don't make noise."

"O.K.," Joey said. "What's a scientist?"

"Scientists mix stuff together to see what will happen." Abby explained. "It's called an experiment."

"Oh," Joey said.

"You get a bowl and some spoons. I'll get stuff out of the refrigerator," Abby said.

"All right," said Joey.

Abby got out bottles and jars and set them on the table next to Joey's bowl. She dumped a thick yellow blob of mustard into the bowl. Then she splashed in some ketchup.

"Stir it," Abby said. "Scientists always stir stuff."

Joey stirred. The experiment turned orange. "Cool," Joey said.

"I'll add more stuff," Abby said. "Scientists always add more stuff."

She plopped in some grape juice. Joey stirred.

Abby added soy sauce, cranberry juice, and mayonnaise.

Joey stirred. The experiment turned a color they had never seen before.

"Is everything all right out there?" Dad called from his office.

"Everything's fine," Abby called back. "Now, let's taste it," she told Joey. "Scientists always taste stuff. If it's food," she remembered to add.

They tasted the experiment. It tasted like something they had never tasted before. "Needs more stuff," Abby said. She added a dash of hot-pepper sauce and some pickle juice. They tasted it again. It made their tongues tingle.

"Much better," said Abby.

Dad came into the kitchen. "It's so quiet in here. What—!" He stopped short and stared.

Abby and Joey looked where Dad was looking. They saw the messy bottles and jars without lids on the table. They saw the blobs of mustard and spots of soy sauce on the chairs. They saw the glob of ketchup on the ceiling.

Abby frowned and thought for a moment. Then she announced, "Time to clean up, Joey. Scientists always clean stuff up."

She got out the mop and a bucket of water and some soap. She and Joey and Dad put away the jars. They mopped and scrubbed and wiped and shined until everything was spick-and-span. As they worked, they talked about what Abby and Joey had put into the mixture. They talked about why the ketchup and mustard turned orange and why the hot-pepper sauce made their tongues tingle.

And they talked about why they should only taste things they know are safe to eat. They were just putting away the mop when Mom dashed in the kitchen door with a bag of groceries in each arm.

"Looks great in here," she said, glancing around. "Now we have to get this chicken barbecued before Grandma gets here."

She spotted the bowl of "experiment" still sitting on the table. "Good," she said, "you already made the barbecue sauce."

"But—," Abby began.

"Try it," Dad said, winking at Abby.

"H'm," Mom said as she lifted a spoonful of the mixture to her lips. "Not bad. Kind of unusual, though. Where did you get the recipe?"

"It was an experiment," Abby explained.

"An original recipe," Dad added.

"Well, never mind," Mom said. "Grandma likes new things. By the way, you two," she added, "I saw that wink."'

Kimi's Ocean

BY DEBRA TRACY

McKenna Montgomery paced around her house, her forehead crinkled in concentration.

"It looks like you have a problem to solve," her mom said, meeting her on the stairs with a load of folded laundry in her arms.

"I do," McKenna replied. "A very important one."

"Want to tell me about it?" Mom asked, setting down the laundry and sitting on the steps.

McKenna sat too. "There's a new girl in our class named Kimi. She's from Hawaii. Yesterday she told the whole class that sometimes she cries herself to sleep because she misses the ocean and the beach so much. I want to help her."

"H'm," Mom said, frowning in thought. "That's a tough one. Especially when there's three feet of snow on the ground. You have your work cut out for you."

But McKenna thought of a solution that very afternoon.

"Mom!" she cried, running excitedly into the kitchen. "Could I have a couple of friends over next Saturday? And can we have your bathroom to ourselves for the whole afternoon?"

"Yes, you may have a couple of friends over. But why do you want to use the bathroom?" Mom asked.

"I'm going to turn it into a beach!" McKenna said, her green eyes sparkling with fun. "Your tub's twice the size of mine. We can pretend it's a mini-ocean. I'll put my seashell collection and your fake pearls in the bottom.

We'll wear our bathing suits and lie on beach towels. We'll have lemonade and chips and egg-salad sandwiches. It will be perfect!"

"I assume you're inviting Kimi?" Mom asked, smiling.

"Of course! The whole thing is for her."

"Sounds like fun," Mom said. "I'll make the sandwiches."

The following Saturday afternoon, Kimi and another friend, Suzette, knocked on the Montgomerys' front door. When McKenna answered it, she laughed. Kimi and Suzette were dressed in winter coats, hats, and gloves, and they were carrying bathing suits and beach towels. McKenna was already in her bathing suit.

"Isn't it a perfect day to go to the beach?" McKenna asked, leading her friends upstairs. "The sun will shine through the skylight and the windows!"

Kimi and Suzette hurriedly dressed in their bathing suits. Giggling, the three friends headed for the large master bathroom. Kimi and Suzette squealed with delight as they walked through the door. "This is just right, McKenna!" they cried.

The tub was filled with blue-tinted water. McKenna had squeezed food coloring into it. On the ocean bottom were shells, pearls, and two plastic starfish that McKenna had bought as souvenirs while on vacation in Florida.

Floating on top of the water were seahorse-shaped sponges. On the floor nearby was a pail, a shovel, and a giant, colorful beachball.

The three friends put on their sunglasses, then spread out their towels and plopped down onto them. The sun shone brightly through the skylight.

"Better put on suntan lotion," McKenna warned. "We might get a sunburn." They helped each other rub coconut-scented lotion on their backs. Then the girls turned onto their stomachs and talked and giggled while eating sandwiches and chips and drinking lemonade.

"This is great!" Kimi said, grinning. She crawled over to the tub to peer into it. "It would be fun to go swimming now."

"It's kind of cold," McKenna said, sticking a toe into their ocean. She added some warm water.

Kimi climbed into the tub first. "It feels like I'm sitting in a little tide pool," she said, her eyes twinkling happily. "Only not as gritty."

Giggling, the other two girls climbed in with Kimi. They splashed and played, squealing as tidal waves swept across their ocean.

"We've been swimming for hours," McKenna finally declared, displaying her pruny fingers. "I wonder if we'll be blue when we get out?"

The girls climbed out of the tub, examining their skin. They were a little disappointed that it wasn't blue.

"Look at the floor!" McKenna exclaimed. "It's covered with water."

"The tide must be coming in," Kimi said. "Let's dry off first. Then we can mop up the water with our beach towels."

"I'm cold," Suzette said when the bathroom floor was dry again.

"Come on," said McKenna, taking both girls by the hand. She led them downstairs to her mom.

"You girls sounded like you were having a lot of fun at the beach today," Mrs. Montgomery said, smiling. "Do you need more lemonade?"

"No thanks, Mom," McKenna answered. "We'd like some hot chocolate, please."

The Good Gift

BY ANN R. BLAKESLEE

As soon as Feodor saw the red brick school building, he liked it. He liked the way it sat flat on the ground with no upstairs. When the doors opened, the children could run right out onto the playground. Soon he would be running and playing with them.

He liked his new classroom too. Goldfish swam in a bowl by the window. Drawings of pumpkins with carved faces smiled or scowled from the walls. And he liked the red-headed teacher who guided him to his seat, her hand warm on his shoulder.

What Feodor didn't like was knowing so few words of English. The ones he'd practiced so hard in Russia didn't sound quite right here in America. His "Please, friend, how are you getting this day?" made people smile. He waited for their answer, but nobody seemed to know what to say.

"It will take time," his father said.

His mother said, "You must be patient, with yourself and with the others. It's hard for everybody." Of course, she said that in Russian. She was having trouble learning English too.

All week Feodor went to the new school. Because he couldn't understand the teacher, he sat and watched what the other children did. After lunch he fought to stay awake; his stomach was so full and his day so empty.

From "The Good Gift" by Ann R. Blakeslee from *Spider* Magazine, September 1995, Vol. 2, No. 9, pp. 8–14. Used by permission.

But on Friday something happened that he could take part in. A lady came to the classroom and made music.

She played an instrument that looked like piano keys fastened to a board. While she played, the children sang. Feodor didn't understand the words, but he hummed along.

At home that night he picked out the school songs on his balalaika. His grandfather had given the instrument to him before Feodor left Russia. His parents hadn't wanted him to bring it.

"They don't play balalaikas in America," his father said. "They play guitars." Feodor knew that was right. Americans were always playing guitars on Russian TV.

"Anyway, how would we pack it?" his mother asked.

"Feodor will carry it," his grandfather said.

"Carry a balalaika all the way to America?" his mother cried.

"Yes," his grandfather said sternly. "Feodor will carry my balalaika to remember Mother Russia by. And to remember me."

Grandfather's balalaika was triangular. It had a long neck. Feodor carried it to the plane wrapped in a baby blanket. But every official they passed made him unwrap it to see what was inside. Finally Feodor left the blanket on a bench.

In the airport crowds, the sharp corners of the balalaika poked people. The long neck caught on pockets and purse straps, and Feodor received many angry looks. Still, he was glad he'd brought the instrument all the way to America. When he played it, he remembered his grandfather. Sometimes he cried, remembering.

"Grandfather," he said, wishing his grandfather could hear him, "it's nice in this new land. Parts of it look just like Russia. But none of it looks like you."

The next Friday Feodor decided to take his balalaika to school. He thought maybe his grandfather had sent him that idea.

Feodor left for school early, before the playground became crowded. He didn't want the sharp corners of his balalaika to poke the children and make them angry.

When the locks on the school door snapped open, Feodor went inside. He showed the balalaika to his teacher. She plucked on its strings and laughed with Feodor at the tinkly sound. Then she put the instrument under her desk to keep it safe.

When the music teacher came, Feodor went and picked up the balalaika. He held it out, and she motioned him to play it. He played a song of Mother Russia, a sad song that told how much he missed his homeland. Although the children clapped politely when he finished, he could see that they were bored.

Grandfather, he thought, what shall I do now?

And in his mind, he thought he heard his grandfather say, "Play the American school songs." So he did. He played, "Row, Row, Row Your Boat," and everybody looked surprised. Then he played "Jingle Bells," and two children sang along. When he played "My Country, 'Tis of Thee," everyone sang. They clapped at the end.

Then it was time for the music lady to leave. The children groaned. Feodor, too, was sorry the lesson was over. But the lady beckoned him to go with her.

When he laid the balalaika down to follow, she made him understand that he was to bring it. She had him play the songs in one classroom after another. All the children sang.

After school Feodor hurried home. He ran upstairs to his apartment and banged on the door. His mother flung it open. "What has happened?" she asked. "Something terrible?"

"No, something wonderful. Listen." He played the school songs on his balalaika, one after the other. As he played, he sang.

"I can't understand a word," his mother said.

"Because it's English," said Feodor. "I played the songs in every classroom. By the time I'd heard them over and over, I could sing the words too."

His mother hugged Feodor and the balalaika both at once. "It's a beginning," she said. "Wait till your father hears."

When his father heard, he said, "Grandfather was right to make you bring the balalaika, even though you had to carry it all the way."

His mother asked Feodor to write Grandfather. "Tell him that the balalaika is helping you learn English," she said.

"Write that the children in the new school like hearing you play it," his father said.

Feodor did as they asked, though he thought maybe Grandfather already knew those things without being told.

The Big Tree

BY BRUCE HISCOCK

The big tree is a sugar maple. It stands high on a hill in northern New York State, by the last farmhouse on a dirt road. Sugar maples are common trees there, but few ever grow to this size.

The massive trunk of the old maple is over four feet thick, and its branches rise a hundred feet in the air. It is a giant tree now and still growing. But of course, it wasn't always so big.

Long ago, around the time of the American Revolution, this tree began as a small seed.

Most of the country was wilderness then, and an ancient forest covered the spot where the farmhouse now stands. Wolves prowled silently in those woods. Eagles glided overhead, and tall evergreens swayed in the wind, brushing their needles against the broad leaves of the hardwood trees.

Some of those hardwoods were maples, and one fall they released thousands of winged seeds.

The seeds whirled and spun as they fell. Some landed on the rocks and some in the brook. One seed, no different from the others, came down on a patch of good soil and was covered by falling leaves.

The seed did not sprout, though, for sugar maple seeds must be chilled by the winter before they are ready to grow. Soon the cold days came, and a blanket of snow pressed the seed to the ground.

From *The Big Tree* by Bruce Hiscock. (Caroline House, an imprint of Boyds Mills Press, 1991). Reprinted with permission of Boyds Mills Press. Text copyright © 1991 by Bruce Hiscock.

In the spring, when the sun warmed the earth, a slender white root pushed out of the seed.

As the root grew into the damp soil, the tiny stem began lifting the seed from the ground.

The seed split open, and a long pair of seed leaves unfolded.

In a few days the true maple leaves appeared, and the big tree was on its way. The year was 1775.

That same spring Paul Revere made his famous ride, and the American colonists began fighting the British. It was the start of the Revolutionary War.

The next summer, as the fighting continued, the Americans declared their independence from England on July 4, 1776. The tree was just a year old. Later a fierce battle was fought in the valley below the hill, but the war never reached the old forest.

The maple grew very slowly during this time, for huge trees sheltered the seedling, keeping the forest floor dark and shady. After six years, the tree was only as tall as a rabbit.

Then one spring, when George Washington was president, a violent storm swept over the hill. It knocked down an old white pine, and for the first time, bright sunshine reached the little maple. The tree began to straighten and lift its leaves toward the light.

The maple grew steadily after that. In a few summers it was much taller than the seedlings in the shade. Like all green plants, the tree was using energy from the sun to make its own food.

The big tree is very old now, but still strong and growing. With a bit of luck, and clean air and water, it will go on shading picnics for many more years.

Into the Volcano

BY CHARNAN SIMON

You're taking us WHERE?" Heidi looked at her parents in horror. In the week they'd been in Hawaii, they'd seen rain forests and waterfalls and beautiful sandy beaches. But this couldn't be right. "Volcanoes are dangerous! Parents don't take their children to volcanoes!"

Heidi's brother David grabbed her from behind and started shaking. "Look out—the volcano is erupting, with fiery hot lava and earth-shattering quakes! I think it's got Heidi!"

Heidi's dad caught her chair before David toppled her. "Enough already, David," he said mildly.

David shrugged and let go. "Anyhow, you've already been to a volcano. This whole island is volcanoes."

Heidi looked doubtfully at David. "He's kidding, right?"

Dad shook his head. "Afraid he's right this time. All the Hawaiian Islands were formed by volcanoes built up from the ocean floor."

Heidi looked out the window of their condominium, at the wide sandy beach and glittery blue ocean. It was hard to believe she was on a volcano. "But they don't explode any more, right?" she asked.

Mom gave Heidi a hug. "We're plenty safe here, honey. But Kilauea, the volcano we're going to see, IS still erupting."

"Come on," Dad said. "It'll be fun. Now grab your hiking boots and let's go."

Once they were in the car, David stopped trying to scare Heidi. "Look, Hawaii really was made by volcanoes, but it happened millions of years ago. The lava flowed out of vents in the earth, and as it cooled it gradually built up into mountains."

Pretty soon they were slowing down to turn. "Here we are," said Dad, "Volcanoes National Park. This road will take us all around Kilauea Crater."

Heidi looked out the window nervously. "The one that's still going off?" she asked.

"Yep." Now David was reading from his guidebook. "It says here Kilauea is the world's most active volcano."

Heidi kept looking, but all she saw was a wide, treeless plain. "Hey!" she said. "The ground's steaming!"

"Cool," David said. He kept reading as Mom got out her camera. "The ground just a few feet down is so hot that tree roots can't survive. Only shallow-rooted grasses and plants grow here. Ground water seeps down to the hot volcanic rocks and returns to the surface as steam."

Gradually the landscape changed. There were deep, dry gullies on either side of the road, and old, cold lava flowed everywhere. Mom's camera clicked and clicked.

"Older lava flows are reddish," read David, "because the iron in them has turned to rust. Newer lava flows are black. Hey—remember those black sand beaches we saw? Those are lava beaches!"

Dad pulled the car over to a lookout point. "Everybody out," he said. "We're at Halema'uma'u, home of Pele, Goddess of Hawaiian Volcanoes."

After just a short walk they found themselves looking across a gigantic hole in the ground.

"Wow!" said David. "That's one big crater!"

Dad agreed. "Less than a hundred years ago, this was a lake of molten lava."

Heidi held her nose. "What smells like rotten eggs?"

"Sulphur dioxide," Mom answered, snapping a picture of the crater. "It's a gas. Volcanoes throw out a lot of gases with all that lava. It does stink, doesn't it?"

"Too much," Heidi said. "Let's go back to the car!"

They hadn't driven far before Mom was focusing her camera again. "Look!" she called from the front seat. "Off to the left. There's Mauna Loa volcano. It's the biggest mountain in the world!"

Heidi looked. "That can't be the biggest!" she protested. "I've seen lots bigger mountains in Colorado."

Dad grinned. "Sure you have. But the trick here is, you can't SEE most of Mauna Loa! Only about a third of the mountain is above sea level. The rest is hidden under the ocean. It's gigantic—the biggest mountain on the planet!"

Now the landscape was changing again. Forest of trees and ferns made everything look lush and green. "The next part of the road is pretty twisty," Dad warned. "We're heading back down to the ocean."

Heidi dozed as they drove. She was dreaming of ice-cream sundaes running with rivers of hot molten fudge when David's yelp woke her up.

"The road's covered with dried lava!" he said.

It was. Just like that, the road ended in a flooding of black, glassy looking lava. "In 1990, lava flows blocked the highway," David read. "Hawaiians have had to rebuild lots of roads because of lava flows."

"Here's where hiking boots come in handy," Dad said, as they left the car and picked their way carefully across the rough, sharp field. "You can't walk on lava with sandals."

Heidi looked. This wasn't the sparkly blue ocean outside her condominium window. This was a witches' cauldron! Huge clouds of steam rose into the sky at the coastline. Below the steam, Heidi could see glowing red lava.

"It's coming out of an underground lava tube," Dad said. "This is how Hawaii is still being built, even today! The lava flows into the ocean, and more lava lands on top of it, and then more and more, until new solid land is built. And when the hot lava hits the ocean, the water turns to steam. Incredible!"

Mom was snapping pictures as fast as she could, and David was using binoculars to get a closer look. Heidi just stood and stared. Volcanoes were awesome and huge and beautiful. They were also scary. She wasn't exactly sorry when they hiked back to the car.

And even David was pleased with the Hot Lava Sundae Heidi made up for their afternoon snack. A mountain of macadamia nut ice cream with hot fudge sauce and cherries flowing down its sides might not make the guide books, but it sure tasted good.

All the Same, Only Different

BY UMA KRISHNASWAMI

"We took the best of two worlds and made one world." —Isabel Singh Garcia, Yuba City, California

"Keep your eye on the penny," says Papi. "Then let it spin. See? That's how we flipped coins when I was a boy in India."

"We played that game, too, in Mexico," says Mami, kneading wheat flour into dough. "I think everybody plays that game."

My penny, newly made in 1927, whirls in great, round arcs. But my little brother Emilio's hands won't do as they are told. He laughs so hard that his penny tumbles madly.

The next day, coming back from school, Emilio does not laugh. Instead his voice quivers with trying not to cry.

"They teased me," he says. "They wouldn't let me play. They said I'm not American. Mami, I *am* American."

Mami washes his hot face.

"*Mi hijo*, be strong. You must be proud inside. Proud of being Indian and Mexican and American all at once."

I want to say, *It happens to me too*. I want to say something that will bring my brother's smile back to his face. Buy my words are not strong enough, proud enough, so I keep them inside.

My father's steel bracelet clinks against a glass of tea. *Ting!* It is a proud sound. I ask, "Papi, will you tell us a story? Tell us the one about why you cut your hair."

And Papi tells a story as long as his hair used to be, once, long ago, when he first came from India to America. He says, "I was a soldier in the Great War. I fought in the deserts of Africa and in the fields of France. But the war ended, and you know that when there is no war, they don't need soldiers anymore. So I thought, I will go back to my home in India, to be a farmer."

"But there was no more land to farm," I say. We know this story well.

"The rains failed," says Papi, "and you know that when there is no rain, there is no work for farmers anymore. So I thought, I will go away, far away to Panama."

"To build a big canal," I say. Emilio's eyes are wide.

"But by the time I got there," says Papi, "the canal was built already, and they did not need workmen anymore. So I thought, I will go to America—to California—where they have big fields and need people to plow and plant and pick."

"So you walked to California!" cries Emilio, his frown melting like ice cream in summer. "And you walked and you walked!"

Papi nods. "I walked and walked, and it got very hot, so I took my turban off. But the sun burned the hair right off my head. It never grew back so long again."

"It's a joke!" cries Emilio. "Papi cut his hair so they'd give him a job in America."

"People didn't understand," says my mother, dusting flour onto a board. "They wouldn't hire someone so foreign, with a turban on his head."

"Papi is not foreign," I say. "He is our Papi." I pinch off a piece of dough. I roll it into soft, fat shapes.

"Are you making Indian rotis or Mexican tortillas?" asks Emilio.

My father says, "Tortillas," and my mother says, "Rotis," at exactly the same time. That's how they are. They speak each other's thoughts.

"Rotillas," says Papi. "Tortis. All the same, only different."

I help Mami roll the small round balls of dough into flat circles.

Emilio takes a penny from the jar. He tumbles it around, and soon he's giggling.

The next day is Sunday, the day all the Mexican-Indian families in the valley gather to sing and pray. Then we spend a lazy afternoon around a table loaded with food—rotis, chicken curry, tortilla soup to bring a sizzle to your ears, cool limeade to put the fire out. The chattering conversations of grandmothers and aunts weave a warm blanket around us.

We toss our pennies. Emilio is getting better at this game. "Look!" He laughs. "My penny shines like the sun."

But soon Sunday is gone, and on Monday, when we come home from school, Emilio's laughter is gone too. Mami sighs. She hugs him, but he rips away.

Again I search for proud words, strong words. Again I cannot find them. But now an angry spark has caught fire inside me. It keeps me up at night. It makes my brain whirl like Emilio's penny.

And in the morning, when Emilio stamps his foot and swears he'll never go to school again, I am ready with a story that has spun its way into my head—a story as long as Papi's hair was, once, long ago, when he first came from India to America.

From the bowl on the kitchen table, I gather up a piece of dough. I roll it into soft, fat shapes.

"Here's a little piece of dough," I say, "and it doesn't know what it wants to be."

"I don't know this story," Emilio complains.

"Of course you don't," I tell him. "How could you? I just made it up." And I begin my story.

"The little piece of dough thinks, I'll be a loaf of bread, soft inside and crusty outside. Butter will melt on me. They will serve me with apple cider and ripe, juicy peaches."

Emilio's eyes get round as pebbles.

"But though it tries and tries, the little piece of dough can't rise the way dough should for bread. Mami, why can't it?"

"It has no yeast in it," she says softly.

I carry on. "The other loaves of bread laugh at it. So it thinks, Maybe I'll be a tortilla, all soft and round with little brown spots. They'll roll me up and serve me with beans and salsa bursting with tomatoes and cilantro."

Emilio's body trembles with listening.

"But though it tries and tries, the little piece of dough can't make a good tortilla. Mami?"

"It's too brown," she says, "with not enough salt."

I continue. "It thinks, I'll be a roti, puffed up over a hot fire like a little pillow. I'll be delicious with potato curry and okra. They will serve me up with yogurt, creamy and cool."

Emilio is still as a summer night.

"But it isn't quite right for a roti." I say. "Mami, why not?"

"It has lime in it," she whispers, "and it's softer than roti dough."

I pause. "Nina," says Mami, "what does the dough decide to be?"

The kitchen fills with the sound of listening.

"A torti," I reply, "or a rotilla. Puffed up like a roti, soft as a tortilla, delicious with anything. Tortis, rotillas, rotis, tortillas. All the same, only different."

Papi says, "The little piece of dough can rise up in the sky and be the sun, if that's what it wants to do."

Emilio feels in his pocket. "Like my penny?" he asks.

My father gathers us all into the big, warm circle of his hug. "Like your penny, *puttar*."

We listen to Emilio's silence, and in it are ten thousand little whispers of hope. Slowly, he picks up his book bag. "You coming?" he asks me.

And he heads for the door, reaching into his pocket as he goes, feeling for his shiny penny that can spin laughter.

The Brand New Kid

BY KATIE COURIC

Ellie McSnelly and Carrie O'Toole
were running and laughing—their first day of school
was today! And they wondered just what was in store.
Would this be a good year? Would school be a bore?

They kept fingers crossed they'd be in the same class,
and on a big table that they had to pass
they checked to find out to which room they should go.
"McSnelly . . . 240, O'Toole, I don't know . . .

Oh, here it is, dear, you're 240 as well."
They squealed with delight, Oh gee, this was swell!
240 meant they would both have Miss Kincaid,
the best teacher by far in the whole second grade.

They took their seats quickly, Miss Kincaid called the roll.
Emily Allen (here!) Tyler Antole . . .
(Here!) Peter Barsinsky, Raquel Brooks (here too!)
She went down the list until she was all through.

Then she got to the boy was not in her book.
"We have a new student" . . . they all turned to look.
"His name is a different one, Lazlo S. Gasky,
he's new to our school and the town of Delasky.
Please welcome him here, won't you all please say hi?"

But the students just turned and stared at the new guy.
His hair was so blond, why it looked almost white.
It stuck out all over, it didn't look right.
His lips were bright pink, his eyes very blue.
He looked at his feet and he fidgeted too.
He was quiet at first and then yelled out, "Hello."
His voice booming so loud it made Ellie say, "Whoa!"
The other kids laughed, gee this new boy was weird.
Too different and strange to fit in they all feared.

"Now, class," Miss Kincaid said, her voice shrill and tight,
"let's focus on learning and getting things right."
She turned from the students, white chalk was her tool
as she wrote, *Welcome Back to Brookhaven School!*

They sharpened their pencils and picked up their books,
all morning long, they kept shooting him looks.
They headed to gym class, a quick softball game,
when they went to pick teams, no one mentioned his name.

At lunch, Ricky Jensen, who thought he was cool,
made everyone laugh when he shouted "Hey fool!"

As Lazlo was leaving the line with his tray
someone tripped him, his food it went every which way.
The students all froze as they saw Lazlo's face
with French fries and ketchup all over the place.

So these first weeks were lonely for this brand new kid.
They made fun of him, all that he said and he did.
So he kept his head bowed and stopped trying to please
and simply prepared for the next taunt and tease.

One day after school Ellie walked out the door
and she saw someone she hadn't seen there before.
A lady whose faced looked so tired and worn,
she had tears in her eyes and she seemed so forlorn.
"Who is that?" Ellie asked of a student she saw.
"Oh, that's Lazlo's mother," said Susie McGraw.
"Her son's having trouble, she might pull him out,
this school may be wrong for him, she's full of doubt."
Ellie watched Mrs. Gasky as she walked toward her car.
She thought about how things were going so far,
about Lazlo and how he felt different and strange
and wondered aloud just what she could arrange.

"I've got it!" she said. "I'll ask him to play
at my house or his after school ends one day."
The next morning she walked up to him at his locker,
"Would you like to come over and maybe play soccer?"

Stunned, he said, "Please come to my house and play."
So Ellie said, "Sure, I can, let's pick a day."
"How about Thursday?" he asked with a smile,
a look that hadn't been on his face in a while.

They walked home from school with their books in their arms,
passing meadows and fields and a couple of farms.
They arrived at his door greeted by his French poodle
and Mrs. Gasky was there with a plate of warm strudel!

As they munched on the pastry, they made quite a mess
and Lazlo said, "Do you know how to play chess?"
Ellie said, "Yes, but I'm not all that great."
"That's okay," he replied and he soon said "Checkmate!"

The afternoon ended, Ellie said, "This was fun."
Lazlo just smiled and said, "Hey, thanks a ton
for coming to my house and being my friend
at a school in a town where I just don't fit in."

At school the next day the kids stopped her and said,
"You were walking with Lazlo, are you sick in the head?"
Ellie paused and replied, "Now I know him, you see,
Lazlo isn't that different from you and from me.
He's terrific at chess, and his Mom's really sweet.
Playing soccer the guy doesn't have two left feet.
He may look slightly strange, have an accent and stuff,
but if you knew him, you'd like him, it wouldn't be tough."

Carrie looked at her friend and she thought for a while
and when Lazlo walked up she gave him a big smile.

"Hey Ellie! Hey Lazlo! Do you want to go play?"
And they all walked outside on a beautiful day.

Happy Birthday, Old Man Winter!

BY JULIE BROOKS HILLER

Tessa woke to the sound of purring snowplows. She tossed aside her quilt and rushed to the window.

"Snow!" Tessa squealed with delight at seeing the white lawn, the white birdbath, the white sidewalk, and the white car (which was actually red underneath the snow). It was the first snow Tessa could remember in a long, long time.

She stuffed her feet into her slippers and dashed to the kitchen. Her nose caught a whiff of banana pancakes before she slid to a stop in front of the wall calendar. Her fingers danced across the days and weeks before finding the right date: December 21.

"Oh," Tessa gasped in awe as she read the words on the calendar. "The First Day of Winter. . . . Mom!"

Tessa's mother set her spatula on the kitchen counter and said, "What is it, sweetheart?"

"Today is the first day of winter!" Tessa's mother peeked at the calendar. "So it is."

"And it snowed!" exclaimed Tessa happily, jumping up and down.

"It sure did! And how fitting that we have snow on Old Man Winter's birthday." "Whose birthday?" asked Tessa.

"Old Man Winter's." Tessa's mother pointed at the winter sky through the kitchen window. "He brings us winter each year, along with the snow."

"Are we having a birthday party for him?" asked Tessa. "That would be fun, wouldn't it? But no, sweetheart," said Tessa's mother, returning her attention to breakfast on the stove. "I'm just too busy today."

Tessa frowned. No birthday party for Old Man Winter? Everyone else gets to have a birthday party. It wasn't fair!

Then Tessa's frown turned into a smile. She had a wonderful idea.

After breakfast, Tessa phoned her best friends, Sarah and Andrew. "Meet me at the playground in fifteen minutes," she told them.

Tessa marched along the snow-covered sidewalk in her purple snowsuit, boots, and mittens and entered the playground through the big metal gate.

Tessa grinned at the sight of her friends—the twins looked so happy swinging high into the air on the wooden play set. Their giggles echoed off the merry-go-round and slides as they leaped from the swings, landing in the soft snow. Tessa ran to greet them.

"Hi, Tessa!" said Andrew.

"What's going on? Why did you want us to meet you here?" asked Sarah.

"Don't you two know what day it is today?"

"It's not Christmas yet," said Andrew.

"And Thanksgiving was last month," added his sister.

"I know! I know!" said Andrew. "It's Tuesday!"

"No! No! No! It's the first day of winter!" Tessa said with a grin.

Sarah and Andrew looked confused.

"It's Old Man Winter's birthday!" exclaimed Tessa.

"Who?" asked the twins at the same time.

"Old Man Winter. And we're going to have a birthday party for him, right here at the playground."

"That's a great idea!" said Sarah. "What should we do first?"

"We'll need to make a cake," Tessa told her friends.

"How are we going to do that?" asked Andrew.

"We'll make him a snow cake," said Tessa.

The three friends got to work. They pushed all of the snow off the slide and piled it in the center of the playground. They brushed the snow from the merry-go-round and added it to the pile. For decoration, the twins stuck pine cones around the edges, and Tessa sprinkled red holly berries on the sides. Soon they were finished with a snow cake almost half as tall as Tessa.

"What about the candles?" asked Sarah.

"I have an idea," said Andrew.

The girls watched as he cleared snow from under the old maple tree and gathered some sticks. When he finished pushing the stick-candles into the top of the snow cake, they all sang "Happy Birthday" to Old Man Winter.

"Blow out the candles!" said Tessa to the sky.

A breeze suddenly swept across the playground, whipping the flag atop the playhouse and blowing a single pine cone off the cake.

Tessa gazed at the sky and whispered, "Happy Birthday, Old Man Winter." She was closing her eyes to make a wish for him—a wish for lots of snow—when a single, sparkling snowflake floated down from a cloud and, ever so softly, kissed Tessa on the tip of her nose.

Twisters!

WRITTEN BY KATE HAYDEN

Twisters can form when cold air meets warm air. The warm air is sucked up in a swirling column called a funnel cloud. It spins at great speed. Twisters contain the most deadly winds in the world.

No one knows what a twister will do next. It can lift up a large truck and smash it to pieces, but leave small objects undamaged.

A twister once picked up a baby and set him down safely 300 feet away. The baby did not even wake up!

There are lots of strange stories about twisters. A twister once blew away a man's birth certificate. The twister carried it 50 miles then dropped it in a friend's garden. Another twister sucked up some roses and water from a vase. It dropped them in another room. But it left the vase on the table.

One twister picked up a jar of pickles and carried the jar for miles without damaging it.

Twisters come in many different shapes and sizes. They can be thin, white, and wispy. Or they can be big, thick, and black.

They can even be in color! If a twister travels across a muddy field, the mud turns it brown and very smelly.

Twisters can grow bigger and faster as they go along. Some look like they have a loop or knot in the middle. Some are wider at the bottom than at the top. Some are shaped like a tube. Others look like a slice of pie.

Read Aloud Anthology

Lots of people have seen a twister from the outside. But only a few have looked inside a twister and survived.

A farmer named Will Keller once looked up into a twister from his underground shelter. Just as he closed the door of his shelter, he saw lots of mini twisters. These mini twisters can rip through a building and slice it to shreds.

Twisters are also known as tornados. There is an area in the U.S. that is called Tornado Alley. It is famous for its deadly twisters. Up to 300 occur there every year between April and July. They kill more than 80 people.

Twisters form during these months as warm air from the south and cold air from the north—right over Tornado Alley.

Twisters are graded from 0 to 5 on a scale called the Fujita Scale. An F0 damages chimneys. An F1 snaps telephone poles. An F2 rips off roofs. An F3 flips over trains. An F4 destroys even strong homes. An F5 leaves few things standing. In 1999, an F5 ripped through Oklahoma City, Oklahoma. It killed 45 people.

People in Tornado Alley are well prepared for twisters. Most of them have an underground shelter outside their home.

Some people in Texas have a fiberglass shelter buried in their backyard. People without a shelter hide in a cellar or small room in the middle of their house.

Gary England is a TV weather reporter in Oklahoma City. When lots of twisters are expected, Gary's team stays on the air for 30 hours or more.

Scientists tell Gary what the weather will be. Gary can then tell viewers. The scientists use a computer to help them forecast twisters. The computer makes a picture that shows where a twister is and how fast it is traveling.

The scientists can tell Gary what they think will happen. But storm trackers on the road know what is actually happening. These people risk their lives to find and follow twisters. Many of them have modern equipment such as a satellite dish.

The trackers tell Gary all about a twister where it is and where it is going. They can even tell him when a twister is brewing.

In the past, people did not know when a twister was coming. Today, the trackers and scientists give people time to find shelter, and hundreds of lives are saved.

Twister facts:

• People in Tornado Alley can check for twisters when they fill their cars with gasoline. Many pumps show the weather forecast on a screen.

• Winds inside a twister can spin around at up to 300 miles per hour.

• In April 1974, 148 tornadoes tore through 13 states in the U.S. Six of them were F5s—the strongest type of tornado.

• In 1994, in Australia, hundreds of fish fell from the sky. This was probably the work of a twister.

• Twisters that suck up sand in deserts are called dust devils.

• A twister can last for any length of time—from a few minutes to an hour.

Ahmed, the Boab's Son

A STORY FROM EGYPT BY ANDY ENTWISTLE

"Ahmed, wake up."

Sensing the worry in his mother's voice, Ahmed sat up quickly and blinked in the darkness. "What's wrong?" he asked. "Is it another earthquake?"

"No, not an earthquake," his mother whispered. "Get up and come with me, but don't wake Maged," she added, nodding toward his younger brother asleep on the mattress next to him.

Ahmed wondered what was wrong. If there were a fire, his mother wouldn't be whispering. Curious, Ahmed pulled on his pants and wriggled into his T-shirt before following his mother into the front room of his family's small, basement apartment on the outskirts of Cairo. He was surprised to see his father still sleeping on the couch. Ahmed's father was the boab, or caretaker, for the building, and by this time he was usually hard at work washing the floors upstairs.

"Your father is sick today, Ahmed," his mother said. "Run next-door and ask Samir to come and help with the chores." Samir was the boab for the next building and a good friend of Ahmed's family.

Ahmed scurried up the steps and ran down the sidewalk, his bare feet slapping on the pavement. Samir was already washing the cars in front of his building.

"*Sabah el kheer,*" Samir greeted him. "A morning of goodness."

"*Sabah el full,*" Ahmed relied. "A morning of flowers." When Ahmed had explained his problem, Samir shook his head. "I'm sorry, Ahmed. I must wash these cars and do my own floors before I can help. I will come as soon as I can."

Ahmed hurried home deep in thought. The people who paid his father to keep their cars clean would be angry if the cars were dirty when they came out to go to their offices. His mother, too, was afraid when Ahmed told her that Samir could not come. "The floors can wait," she said, "but what about the cars?"

"I will do them," Ahmed said. "I watch Father all the time. They will not be as clean as when he does them, but when the people see that we tried, they will not be too angry, I hope."

"Your father cleans eight cars every morning, Ahmed, and you are only nine years old. Can you do that?" his mother asked.

"He must," Ahmed father's said from the couch, pulling himself up on his elbow. "I promised to keep them clean. Today he will help me keep my promise." He reached out his hand to Ahmed. "Do a good job, my son. Make me proud."

Ahmed got the cleaning supplies from the garage and lugged them to the curb in front of the building where the cars were parked. Ahmed couldn't lift the pail when it was full of water, so he had to take it to the street empty and then drag the hose to the pail.

When it was full, he shut off the water. Then he dipped his sponge in the water and began to clean the first car, wiping away the dust that blew into the city from the desert each night. He wasn't tall enough to reach the roof, but he hoped the owners would understand.

His father cleaned eight cars every morning, but Ahmed was tired after cleaning just one. He wiped away the dust— back and forth, up and down. By the time he finished the second car, his arms felt as if they were about to fall off. Back and forth, up and down. The sun was up before Ahmed finished the third car. Soon the owners would be coming out, but he simply couldn't work any faster. Back and forth, up and down.

The owner of the fourth car came out just as he finished wiping it. "*Sabah el kheer,* Mr. Naguib," Ahmed greeted him.

"Good morning, Ahmed. Where is your father today?" "He is sick," Ahmed replied. "My work is not as good as his, but I am doing my best."

"You are doing a fine job, Ahmed," said Mr. Naguib.

"My car is very clean." Smiling, he took an Egyptian pound from his wallet and handed it to Ahmed. "This is for your good work," he said.

"Thank you, Mr. Naguib," Ahmed said, his eyes wide. He had never had a whole Egyptian pound of his own before. He was still looking at it as the businessman drove away.

Samir walked up to him. "I'm ready to help now," he told Ahmed. "I'll finish the cars and do the floors. Go and have your breakfast. You should be proud of the good job you've done."

Ahmed ran back to his apartment and showed his parents the money. "You earned that money with hard work," his father said from the couch." Thank you for helping me keep my promise."

Ahmed still had the money in his hand as his mother laid out a breakfast of beans, cheese, and bread on the table. "You must be hungry," she said.

But Ahmed didn't answer her—he was fast asleep, dreaming of the things he could buy with his new Egyptian pound.

Bringing Back Salmon

BY JEFFREY RICH

This was a big day for my students at Shasta Union Elementary School in northern California. They would be trying to bring Chinook (shih-NOOK) salmon back to nearby Middle Creek.

This creek flows into a big river called the Sacramento. And for 50 years, there had been no salmon at all in the river or the creeks that flow into it. Why? Because people had changed the flow of the river and had polluted the water. Fewer and fewer salmon were able to survive, and finally they all died out.

Since then, people have solved some of the problems that were killing the fish. So now my students would release more than 100 tiny salmon into the creek. They knew that salmon are amazing travelers. The tiny fish, they hoped, would swim about three miles down the creek to the Sacramento River. Then they would swim 200 more miles to the Pacific Ocean. For two to five years, the salmon would eat and grow. Finally, when they were ready to have young of their own, they'd turn around and swim all the way back upstream to Middle Creek.

Or at least, that's what was supposed to happen. No one knew for sure whether our little fish would ever return to where we'd released them.

Scientists have always wanted to bring salmon back to this area. So when I had found out they needed some help, I had asked my students if they wanted to join in. The kids said, *Yes!*

"Bringing Back Salmon" by Jeffrey Rich. Reprinted from the October 2003 issue of *Ranger Rick*® magazine, with permission of the publisher, the National Wildlife Federation®.

To begin our project, my students visited a fish hatchery. There, they got a bunch of salmon eggs to raise. Salmon can live only in cold water. So the kids kept the eggs in a tank in a refrigerator. They checked the eggs every day.

The kids really enjoyed watching what happened. When the young were ready to hatch, they released an enzyme (a special chemical) that weakened the egg shells. Then the fish wiggled out of their shells and lay on the bottom of the tank.

Baby salmon have yolk sacs attached to their bellies. The sacs are like little bags of high energy food that the babies use to grow. Finally, when the sacs are gone, the fish are ready to eat tiny animals and plants in the water. When that happened to our fish, we knew it was time to release them.

At the creek, the students took one last look at their baby fish. Then they sent them on their way. We watched them swim off and wished them well. Then, on our way back to school, we picked up litter we saw along the creek and the pathway.

Each fall for three years, my students went to the hatchery for more eggs. They eagerly raised and released the baby fish just as they did the first time. Then one day, something wonderful happened. Our fish started coming back! For the first time in 50 years, grown-up salmon were swimming in Middle Creek. The kids had done it! They'd helped to bring these fish back home.

Zooks

BY BRIANNA R.

I wanted a dog since the third grade, when my best friend, Irene, got a chocolate Labrador puppy. As an only child, I thought a puppy was exactly what I needed—a constant companion, playmate, foot warmer, that sort of thing. Unfortunately, my mom was of the belief that small, low-maintenance animals, such as goldfish, made wonderful pets.

"Fish are very rewarding to care for," she often replied to my repeated pleas. But I knew that fish did only three things: swim, eat, and get stuck in the water filter. No, a dog was what I wanted, and I had resolved to fight for one until I succeeded. Finally, one warm April morning, my hard work paid off. Mom and I made a deal.

"A dog is a huge responsibility," she began. "I need you to prove to me that you'll be responsible in handling a dog before I even consider allowing you to get one. You'll need to do a little petsitting."

"Petsitting? Mom, I'm around Irene's dog every day! I'm almost her second owner! I even taught her how . . ."

". . . to shake," Mom finished for me. "You've told me that before. But Irene's dog is full grown and already trained. We're talking about an untrained, energetic puppy. I've gotten you a petsitting job with Ms. Baxter and her new puppy."

"Ms. Baxter? Since when has she had a dog?"

"She got a golden retriever puppy about a week ago. At a party a few days ago, he was something of a nuisance. For her party next week, she wants someone who will play with him. That's all you have to do. And if Ms. Baxter gives me a good report, then you can get a puppy."

"Really?" I asked incredulously.

"Really," she said, smiling.

A week later, I found myself ringing the doorbell of Ms. Baxter's large house.

"Hello, Eileen," Ms. Baxter said as she opened the door. At her feet sat an adorable puppy, which promptly waddled over and began attacking my shoelaces.

"This is Zooks," she said, gesturing toward the puppy. "And if you'll follow me, I'll show you where you need to keep him." I gently pried Zooks off my sneakers and went with Ms. Baxter into the living room, followed closely by the puppy, who still seemed very interested in my laces.

"Zooks has already been fed, so all I want you to do is play with him and keep him in here until dinner is over," she informed me.

Ding-dong! The doorbell rang.

"That must be Mr. and Mrs. Mango, so if you'll excuse me . . ." Ms. Baxter left the room to greet her guests. Zooks attempted to follow her, but I grabbed his collar. "Sorry, buddy," I said. "You'll have to hang out with me tonight."

I played with Zooks for about an hour. When it began to get dark, he crawled over to his basket, curled up, and looked as though he was ready for a long sleep. Feeling fatigued, I threw myself onto the couch and flipped on the television.

A few minutes later, my eyelids began getting droppy. I longed to doze off, but it didn't seem right to nap on the job. In fact, it occurred to me that it probably wasn't a great idea to be watching television on the job, either. I flipped the TV off and glanced at Zooks's basket.

It was empty.

"Zooks?" I called softly, looking around the room. He wasn't there.

If I were a dog, I thought, *where would I go? Somewhere with food and people and . . .*

The dining room!

I crept quietly through the dark kitchen and peered through the doorway of the dining room. Six dinner guests sat at the large mahogany table, apparently absorbed in a highly amusing story Ms. Baxter was telling. They were too absorbed, it seemed, to notice what I noticed—Zooks was crawling around under the table!

Maybe I could get Zooks out before anyone noticed. After all, if he had passed through the room unseen, why couldn't I? Perhaps I could get under the table, snatch Zooks, and sneak out. I got down low on all fours and crawled stealthily toward the table.

"Eileen, what in heaven's name are you doing?" asked Ms. Baxter.

My face grew very hot. Slowly, I lifted my head to look at the seven people who were staring at me. I opened my mouth, but no sound came out.

"Well?" asked Ms. Baxter. I was saved the trouble of answering by a bloodcurdling shriek.

"AHHHHHHHHHHHHHHH!!!"

Chaos! Everyone jumped up in confusion. I saw the source of the scream: one guest's feet were being attacked by Zooks. I sprang into action. Diving under the table, I maneuvered through the fray of feet and grabbed Zooks. Then, still holding the squirming puppy, I backed out from beneath the table.

The commotion had ceased, followed by complete silence. I didn't have the courage to look up at the seven pairs of eyes looking right at me. So, still staring down at Ms. Baxter's white carpet, I began my apology.

"Um . . . I'm Eileen and this is Zooks and I was supposed to be watching him, but um . . . I was careless and let him escape. I'm sorry for the . . . trouble this caused."

I looked up tentatively, waiting for a reprimand or at least some sort of affirmation that they had heard me. But all I saw were seven faces with their mouths open, wearing identical expressions of shock. I tried not to laugh, but I couldn't help myself. I giggled and giggled, and soon everyone in the room was laughing too. Zooks barked in the midst of the racket we were making. Then I suddenly realized that by letting Zooks escape, I had probably just lost my only chance at getting a dog. That wiped the grin right off my face.

A few days later, there was a knock on the door. My mother answered it, and I saw Ms. Baxter standing in the doorway, holding Zooks on a leash.

"Hello, Ms. Baxter! Please come in," Mom said.

"Thank you." Ms. Baxter stopped through the doorway, followed by Zooks, his tail wagging furiously at the sight of me.

"I just have a few things for Eileen," Ms. Baxter went on. She rummaged around in her purse and produced a crisp five-dollar bill. "For your pet-sitting services," she said, holding it out to me.

"Thank-you," I replied, taking it. Then Ms. Baxter held out Zooks's leash.

"Do you want me to take Zooks for a walk?" I asked, puzzled.

"No, Eileen. I want you to have Zooks. Keep him. As your pet."

When these words had sunk in, all I could say was "Huh?"

"After having Zooks for a couple weeks, I've come to think that a puppy isn't the right sort of pet for me," Ms. Baxter continued. "I need a small, low-maintenance animal, like a goldfish. But as I'm still very fond of Zooks, I wanted to give him to a kind, responsible owner."

I glanced at Mom, waiting for her to say something like, "After Eileen's petsitting incident, I'm convinced that she isn't responsible enough for a dog." But she didn't. In fact, she said, "Eileen, aren't you going to thank Ms. Baxter for her generous gift?"

"Thanks," I said weakly, taking the leash. Ms. Baxter smiled, said good-bye, and left. As soon as she was gone, I turned to Mom.

"What . . . who . . . how did this happen?" I stammered at Mom.

"Oh, I don't know," she said mysteriously and then smiled. I immediately suspected conspiracy.

"Can you at least tell me why you let me keep Zooks? I was totally irresponsible at my petsitting job!" I cried.

"Well, after you let Zooks escape, you owned up to your mistake and apologized. If that's not responsibility, then I don't know what is."

"Oh," I said. Things made a little sense now. "Thanks, Mom." I gave her a hug.

I bent down and pried Zooks off my shoelaces.

"Now, Zooks," I said, setting him down. "I'm going to teach you how to shake."

Meet the Author:

Brianna R.

Unlike Eileen, I've had great luck with dogs I've known. When my yellow Labrador, Wisty, was a puppy, she was never as mischievous as Zooks. And my petsitting experiences were never as crazy as Eileen's—the dogs I sat for were always really good!

Brianna, age 13, lives in Virginia

Oscar the Puppy

BY JULIA NASSER PADGETT

Last year Manuel and his dad visited their local animal shelter. They looked at all of the animals in the cages: huge, furry dogs; small orange cats; even some bright green parakeets! Then Manuel walked to a cage in the corner. Inside was a brown, fluffy puppy. He ran around in circles and barked when he saw Manuel. Manuel adopted him and named him Oscar.

As Manuel and his dad drove home with Oscar, they talked about the responsibility of having a pet. "Taking care of a puppy is a big job," Manuel's dad said. "You have to train it and care for it properly."

Manuel understood what his dad meant the minute they got home. After Oscar ran in the door, he chewed on Manuel's mom's shoe. As soon as Manuel took the shoe away from him, Oscar saw Rocky, the family's cat. *Whoosh!* Oscar took off and chased Rocky into the kitchen. By the time Manuel caught up with them, Rocky was under the table, his fur standing up and eyes wide. Then Oscar went to the bathroom on the floor by the refrigerator. Manuel couldn't believe how much trouble a little puppy could get into!

Manuel spent the next few months training Oscar, but it wasn't easy. Oscar loved to chew on everything—shoes, blankets, furniture—so Manuel's dad suggested he give Oscar other things to sink his teeth into. Manuel got an empty shoebox from the basement and filled it with toys and rawhides. After a while, Oscar left everyone's shoes alone and chewed on his own things.

Oscar didn't like being home alone when Manuel and his family were at school and work. He barked and cried as soon as they walked out the door. Manuel asked Oscar's veterinarian how he could help Oscar. The veterinarian told Manuel that every morning before school he should rub Oscar's favorite toy with his hands so that the toy will smell like him. Then Oscar would feel as though Manuel is with him throughout the day.

Manuel and his mom took Oscar on two walks every day, one before school and one after school. Manuel learned how to train Oscar while walking him on a leash. Oscar learned to listen to Manuel's commands. If Oscar tried to run ahead, Manuel said, "Heel, Oscar!" Oscar knew this meant he had to slow down. Soon Manuel and Oscar felt confident on their walks.

By Oscar's first birthday, he was much bigger than he was when Manuel adopted him. Because Manuel took care of and trained Oscar, Oscar was much better behaved, too!

Bear and Duck on the Run

BY JUDY DELTON

Duck knocked on Bear's door. "Come in," called Bear in a sleepy voice. "What are you doing here in the middle of the night?"

"It isn't nighttime, Bear," said Duck. "It's morning. And I have something for you. I found a pair of running shorts just your size at Mockingbird Mall."

"Why, thank you, Duck," Bear said, stretching his legs. "But what do I need running shorts for?"

"You need exercise, Bear," said Duck. "Exercise is good for the heart, you know. And it can help you lose weight. You are a large bear," he added kindly. "Now that you have running shorts, we can run together. Why, I run three miles every day. Put on your shorts, and we'll begin at once."

Bear frowned. "Duck, I don't think these running shorts will fit. They look too small."

"Why," said Duck, "I'm sure I got the correct size. Put them on," he demanded. "Let me see how they fit."

Bear sighed. He pulled the shorts on over his pajamas. "See?" he said. "They are too tight."

"Bear, you don't put shorts on over pajamas! Take your pajamas off."

Without pajamas, the shorts fit perfectly. Duck rubbed his wings together. "Let's hit the road. The early bird catches the worm."

When they were outside, Duck said, "My daily run is to the fish store in the village and back again. Now, Bear, I will run ahead and wait for you at the fish store. Then we'll start back together."

Duck waved and was out of sight before Bear had taken one step.

Bear began to run. He ran for three minutes. Then he sat down to rest. He wiped his face with a handkerchief.

Just then Groundhog drove up in his yellow taxicab. He parked it under a tree and got out.

"Good morning, Bear. Have a doughnut?" he said, opening a brown bakery bag.

"Why, thank you, Groundhog. I am rather hungry after my run." "I didn't know you were a runner," said Groundhog.

"Running is good for the heart," said Bear, sighing. He took a large bite of his doughnut.

Bear ate three more doughnuts after Groundhog had left. Then he lay down. He felt warm and tired.

After a while he heard an angry voice. "Bear, I waited and waited, and you didn't come."

Bear looked up. There was Duck standing with his wings on his hips. "I needed a little rest, Duck. It's a long way to the village."

"Nonsense," said Duck, pulling Bear to his feet. "You need to move. We'll try again tomorrow." The next morning Duck heard a low moan from Bear's bedroom. He ran to see what it was.

"OOOHH," moaned Bear. "Just look, Duck. I have a red rash. I won't be able to run today. I must have the measles." Bear put a paw up to his forehead. "I just need lots of rest, Duck. The worst thing you can do when you have measles is run, you know."

Duck hurried into the kitchen and made Bear some soup. He dashed back to Bear's bed. The soup spilled onto the sheets and all over Bear.

"Ouch!" Bear yelled. "Oh my," said Duck. He grabbed a towel and began to wipe the soup off Bear. As Duck wiped, the red spots came off, too.

"BEAR!" shouted Duck. "These spots are painted on! You don't have measles at all."

"For goodness sakes," murmured Bear. "I must have gotten berry stains on me when I had my breakfast this morning."

"Get out of bed right now, Bear," Duck said finally, "and we'll start our run."

"Now," said Duck, slapping Bear on the back, "we will have a race, Bear. I will run to the fish store and back two times while you run there and back only once. You have the advantage. We will meet back here. And the winner," said Duck, "will—"

"Will never have to run again," finished Bear. Duck knew the chances of Bear winning were very slight. "All right," he agreed. "Get set, GO!"

Duck was off like lightning. Bear whistled as he walked along the path.

Before long Groundhog came by in his taxicab. "Groundhog," Bear called, "can you drive me to the fish store on the back road?"

"Why, yes, Bear. Climb in!" said Groundhog. At the fish store Bear bought a brook trout. Then he asked Groundhog to take him home by the back road.

At home Bear took two teacups and a fresh honey cake from the cupboard and put them on the table. He sat down to wait for Duck.

Soon Duck came along the path. He was wiping his face with his handkerchief.

"Come in, Duck, and have some tea and cake," Bear called to him.

"Why, Bear! What are you doing here ahead of me?"

"As you can see," said Bear, "I am the winner. I got back here before you did, Duck. I went to the fish market and bought this fine trout for my dinner." He poured tea for both of them and offered Duck some cake. Then Bear felt guilty. "Duck," he said, "I did go to the fish store. But I went in Groundhog's taxi."

Duck looked surprised. "You cheated, Bear! You didn't run at all!"

"I hate to run, Duck."

Duck sighed. He took a bite of honey cake. "This is delicious," he said. "You are a very good cook, Bear. I guess we can't all be athletes."

Bear smiled. "Give these to your new running partner," he said, handing Duck the shorts. "I hope you find someone who *likes* to run."

Eat Your Vegetables

BY JAMES MARSHALL

An owl, who had decided to spend the morning in bed, was fluffing up her pillows when she heard the most awful noise from outside. It was the sound of munching. And it was coming closer.

"Termites!" cried the owl. "They must be gigantic!"

But when she stepped out her front door, she saw what was up. And it wasn't termites. A brontosaurus was merrily eating the oak tree in which the owl made her home.

"Delicious," said the brontosaurus. "I really think I prefer oak to elm. Although an occasional hickory is a nice alternative."

"May I ask what you think you are doing?" said the owl.

"I'm having my breakfast," replied the brontosaurus calmly. "If you don't mind."

"I do mind," said the owl. "This is my home. Go find breakfast someplace else."

"I'll do no such thing," said the brontosaurus. "You'll simply have to relocate."

And he opened his ferocious jaws and took another bite.

"That's my terrace!" shrieked the owl. "I'm warning you!"

The brontosaurus found this amusing.

"Oh yes?" he said. "Just what do you intend to do about it?"

"You'll see," said the owl.

And she hurried inside to make emergency calls to all her friends.

"Stop everything and get over here at once!" she cried. "There isn't a second to lose!"

The brontosaurus didn't give the owl another thought and continued with his breakfast. He hummed a little tune as he chewed. Suddenly he heard the sound of flapping wings. Before he knew it, the oak tree was covered with birds—sparrows and larks, hawks, gulls and crows, finches, hummingbirds, buzzards and canaries. They were perched on every branch. They looked defiant.

"Out of my way!" roared the brontosaurus.

But the owl's friends would not budge. The brontosaurus tried to find an empty branch to nibble on, but everywhere he looked a bird was stationed.

"You'll have to eat us along with the leaves and branches," said the owl.

"Ugh!" cried the brontosaurus. "What a disgusting thought. You know I'm a vegetarian!"

"I'm nice and bitter," said one of the crows.

"I'm on the slimy side myself," said a pigeon.

The brontosaurus felt his stomach turning a little queasy.

"I'm good and salty," said a plump gull.

"Stop that!" roared the brontosaurus.

"I hope you don't mind a few bones with your buzzard," said one old bird.

By now the brontosaurus felt positively nauseated. But although his appetite was ruined, he didn't want to lose face.

"I believe I hear someone calling me," he said. "We'll continue this discussion some other time."

And he lumbered away and out of sight.

"Nice work," said the owl to the other birds.

"Some problems we just can't manage alone," said the buzzard. "And it's wonderful to have friends to whom we can turn in a crunch."

"You said a mouthful," said the owl.

The Hoot and Holler Hat Dance

A FOLK TALE FROM GHANA RETOLD BY LAURA S. SASSI

Anansi, the spider, was once very handsome, with eight long legs, a round little belly, and a stunning head of hair. He was also very greedy and hoarded everything in sight. Alas, his never-ending appetite eventually cost him his hair.

It happened at harvesttime. "Make yourself useful, dear, and go help your mama pick the corn," Anansi's wife said to him one morning as he lounged lazily in his web.

"Ugh," Anansi groaned, for the mere mention of work made his tummy growl. Nevertheless, he grabbed his hat and started slowly on his way.

To his dismay, the path was hot and dusty, and tasty tidbits were few and far between. Only the thought of Mama's delicious bean stew kept him going.

By the time he arrived, all he could think about was spicy beans simmering in Mama's famous stew. "I want to eat!" he hollered as he pushed open the gate.

"Not till you finish picking the corn!" Mama exclaimed. Then, handing him a basket to fill, she scurried back to the kitchen.

"The Hoot and Holler Hat Dance" by Laura S. Sassi. Reprinted by permission of *Spider* magazine, November 2004, Vol. 11, No. 11, copyright © 2004 by Carus Publishing Company.

Soon, the field was filled with the aroma of Mama's beans and onions. To his credit, Anansi tried to ignore the smell. First he turned this way, then he turned that. Still, the wonderful fragrance swirled all around him. "I must eat!" he panted, putting down his basket.

Just then, Mama crossed the field with a calabash bowl. "Stew at last!" he rejoiced, as he gulped his first mouthful. Then he spat, for it was only water!

"We'll feast when you finish," Mama scolded.

But Anansi could bear it no longer. When Mama disappeared, he dashed to the kitchen. The bean stew hissed and bubbled in the pot. "Mmm!" Anansi cried. In seconds he was greedily guzzling spoonful after spoonful.

But little spoonfuls were not enough. "I want more!" he belched. Yanking off his hat and turning it upside down, he filled it to the brim.

Just then he spotted Okra, the cat. "Uh-oh!" Anansi yelped, quickly plopping his bean-filled hat on his head. Then he smiled his handsomest smile.

"Greetings, Anansi," Okra purred politely. "What are you doing here?"

"Just helping dear old Mama with the harvest," Anansi replied with syrupy sweetness.

But he didn't feel sweet. He felt hot, so hot it hurt! He shook his hat a little, but the boiling beans still burned. He shook his hat a little faster, but the stew still scalded. He jumped. He danced. He jiggled his hat. Still, the beans burned hotter and hotter.

Sensing a commotion, Kraman, the dog, appeared. "What is wrong with you?" he woofed.

"Nothing!" Anansi hollered. "Don't you know? It's Hat-Shaking Day!"

"Never heard of it," Kraman barked.

"Why, yes!" Anansi shouted, shaking his head faster and faster.

"It happens once a year! Hat-Shaking Day!

Ha—Ha—Hat-Shaking Day!" Anansi sang, hooting and hollering down the path. Finally, he could stand it no longer. With one final howl, he ripped off his hat.

Okra and Kraman roared with laughter as beans and onions spilled everywhere. Soon the birds and bugs joined in, for greedy Anansi was quite a sight. The beans had completely burned off his hair, leaving him as bald as a corn kernel!

Alas, his hair never grew back. That is why to this day, Anansi shuffles in shame through the grass, where no one can see his big, bald head.

Troublemaker

BY JODI WHEELER

In second grade, I was the troublemaker in Mrs. Kirk's class, and everybody knew it. When I got into an argument over whose turn it was on the swing, kids in my class whispered, "Stay away from Justin. He's a troublemaker." All of the teachers knew me, too. When I ran through the halls, I could hear them saying, "Watch that one. He's a troublemaker."

But in third grade, Mrs. Richardson was my teacher. She met us at the door on the first day and showed each of us to a seat. We had to fill out cards saying what we wanted to be when we grow up. I didn't know what to write, so I looked around the room. On the wall next to me was a poster of a tall man with sharp, dark eyes. It read "Langston Hughes, great American poet." On my card I wrote: Justin Flinn, poet.

Mrs. Richardson collected the cards and looked through them. "Justin!" she exclaimed. "You want to be a poet. How wonderful." My best friend, Ray, started laughing, and several others joined in, but Mrs. Richardson interrupted them. "I'm sure that Justin writes very nice poetry. Hopefully we can get him to share some of it with us soon."

The laughter stopped, but I sank down in my chair. Share some of it? I'd never written a poem in my life.

The next morning, Mrs. Richardson greeted me at the door again and said, "I'm looking forward to reading some of your poetry."

When I got to my desk, I pulled out some paper. I was stuck. I was going to have to find a way to write a poem. At the top of the page I wrote "School."

"I go to school," I wrote for the first line. What rhymes with school? Fool, drool, cool . . . . "School is cool," I added. That was silly. I wadded the paper up and shoved it aside. As I tried to come up with a new start, Ray nudged my arm.

"Hey, Justin," he whispered. "Throw that paper ball at Nieka."

"*Sssh*, I'm busy," I answered.

"Aw, come on," he whispered again. "It'll be funny."

I ignored him and kept trying to figure out what kind of poem to write.

"Fine. I'll do it myself," Ray said.

As I concentrated on my poem, Ray tossed the paper across the room. *Smack!* It hit Nieka on the forehead.

Mrs. Richardson turned around to see where the paper had come from. She looked me straight in the eye and said firmly, "Justin, we are not going to have that kind of behavior in this class. Move your desk to the back of the room and face the wall."

"But it wasn't—" I tried to protest.

She pulled my desk to the back. "Here's a work sheet for you to do while the class does an activity. I'll let you know when I think you're ready to join us again."

I grabbed my chair and shoved it over to my desk.

I snatched a notebook from my book bag and yanked out a piece of paper. If she wants me to be a paper thrower, I can be a paper thrower, I thought as I balled the paper into a tight wad. I turned around in my seat and eyed Ray. He was hard at work on his assignment.

Suddenly I knew that all Mrs. Richardson would see was that Ray was hard at work and I was causing trouble.

I twisted back around and put my head on my desk. I was so mad! I wanted to turn around and yell that it wasn't fair and I didn't do it. I smoothed out my paper. I wrote MAD and stared at the letters for a moment before I began to fill in the lines next to them.

By the time I had finished writing, I felt better. And I had an idea. I did the work sheet as quickly as I could and then got out a clean sheet of paper and wrote:

Dear Mrs. Richardson,

This year I am not a troublemaker. I am a poet.

My fists tighten, and my head hurts

As I try not to yell that I

Did not throw the paper!

Please, can I move my desk back to where it belongs?

Justin

As I signed my name, Mrs. Richardson started calling groups to line up for recess. She called me last, but instead of lining up, I brought my paper to her.

She looked at the paper with surprise. "Justin, I'm so sorry!" she exclaimed. "Thank you for telling me in such a mature way. We'll move your desk as soon as we get back from recess."

I couldn't believe that it had actually worked!

I could stick to this poetry business. As we walked down the hall, I came up with an idea for another poem. I'd write one about Mrs. Richardson. While I jotted my idea down on a scrap of paper, I heard a teacher pointing me out to Mrs. Richardson, saying, "You'd better watch out for that boy."

"Oh yes," said Mrs. Richardson. "I know all about Justin. He's a poet."

The Princesses Have a Ball

BY TERESA BATEMAN

Once upon a time, not so long ago, there were twelve sweet princesses all in a row. Though their dad was short and they were growing tall, and the king remarked, "This won't do at all! Why, to catch a prince you should be petite, dance and walk with grace, and have tiny feet."

But they didn't dance, as a point of pride, and their dainty step was a healthy stride.

Then one morning when the girls took their place, every princess shoe was a pure disgrace. With the satin ripped, and the ribbons torn, and the instep stripped, and the sole all worn.

"What goes on at night? What do you girls do, that would wear a hole into every shoe? You should be asleep," fussed the king, "I say—dreaming of a prince and your wedding day."

Princesses should not have their toes in view. So new shoes were bought—they were ruined too! For the next three weeks it went on that way, with their shoes worn out each and every day.

"Now I've had enough," said their dad, "I fear there is something strange going on 'round here."

So the puzzled king sent out a decree asking for a key to this mystery. Soon the halls were filled with detectives whose only mission was to explain those shoes.

One believed disguise would reveal the truth, but the girls caught on and threw out that sleuth! And another hoped he could track them down, but the girls made friends with his well-trained hound. There were spies, and traps—but no clever plot could outwit those girls. They would not be caught!

Now a man named Jack, of the cobbler trade, saw the ragged shoes that the king displayed. Jack remarked, "It's strange, but it's clear to me that these shoes were worn out athletically."

Jack just had to know how the deed was done, so he crept passed guards as the clock struck one. In the princesses' room he was not surprised to see empty beds that had been disguised. Through the closet door, standing open wide, lay a passageway, so Jack went inside. Then a *thump-thump-thump* shook the passage walls, and he tiptoed up and saw BASKETBALLS?

In a basement room, as the night grew short, were a dozen girls on a makeshift court. They made up two teams, with two substitutes. And they ran and passed and they shouted, "SHOOT!"

When the game was done and the girls were through, there was not a sole left on any shoe. Jack slipped silently out the way he came—for he knew a way to improve their game. He designed a shoe with a rubber sole, and a high-topped edge to stop ankle roll. He put arch supports in the proper places, and ditched pink ribbons for sturdy laces.

When the order came for new princess shoes, Jack packed up the ones that he hoped they'd choose. When he placed the shoes on the palace floor, all the girls went, "OOH! Could you make us more?"

Then the youngest said, with her eyes aglow, "How did you find out? Tell me, how'd you know?"

"I can hold my tongue," Jack replied. "But, hey! Why not tell your dad? He should see you play!"

She looked glum. "I doubt he'd give us a chance when he thinks a 'ball' is a kind of dance!"

Jack just smiled and said, "All you girls are strong, don't you think it's time that you proved him wrong?"

Then she grinned, "Hey girls! Let's put on a show!"

When they heard her plan, they were all gung ho!

So they asked the king, on his royal throne, "Can we plan a ball of our very own?"

Then they locked the door to the ballroom tight, and they worked inside morning, noon, and night. When the day arrived for their special ball, guests were quite surprised when they saw the hall. As they took their seats in their fancy dress, they all looked around for their hostesses.

Then a bell rang out, and in shirts and shorts, princesses appeared up and down the court. They were crisp and clean as they showed their skills, dribbling up and down, running passing drills. And they played a game that the crowd adored as they spun and passed, as they shot and scored. All the people's cheers filled the castle hall.

"This is something new! It's a *basket*-ball!"

Then the king stepped down from his royal throne, and he said, "My girls, I wish I had known. Even royalty is allowed some fun, and I'm proud of you, each and every one."

Now their lives is just as the girls would choose. They all play the game—Jack designs their shoes. Since the referee also needs a pair, there are special shoes for the king to wear. And the princesses get their sleep at night—playing games by day to their hearts' delight.

Yankee Doodle Shortstop

BY HELEN J. HINTERBERG

"I HATE BASEBALL."

"You love baseball."

Meg sighed. "I love it and I hate it, I guess."

Her mother was spooning strained peas into Meg's baby brother, Charles. "Don't worry, honey. It'll work out. You made the team."

Meg traced a pattern on the tablecloth with her finger. "What's the point anyway? Girls can't play in the major leagues. Might as well give it up now before I waste any more time."

Mrs. O'Malley sat down at the table and met Meg's unhappy gaze. "I know there's not professional baseball for women, honey. I knew it when I was your age. I played anyway. I loved it."

Meg smiled for the first time that day. "You still play."

"You bet I do. I'm the best darn player in the coed, over-35 league. I carry my team. And I still love it. Now, do me a favor and sing 'Yankee Doodle' to your brother. It'll get your mind off your problems and it'll get more peas into Charles."

Charles was thirteen months old. "Yuckee Doodoo" was his favorite song. It always cheered him up. Meg had sung it to him so many times that singing it was as easy as breathing.

Launching into it now put a wet grin on Charles's face, but it didn't keep Meg from thinking about baseball.

If she didn't love it so much, she would walk away from it without a backward glance. But she loved every single thing about it, from the uniforms that never fit quite right, to the mouthful of dust she inhaled every time she slid into a base; from the painful sting in her hand when a line drive slammed into her glove, to the fierce jolt that leaped up her arm when she hit a ball hard.

She loved all that but she hated being the first girl to play for the Rutledge Falcons and she hated being the worst player on the team.

She had made the team all right, but if she wanted to be accepted as a Falcon, she was going to have to go from worst player to best player in a very big hurry.

The next day, as she took up her position at shortstop, she glanced over at Jamie Ferguson on first base. He didn't smile but he gave her a quick thumbs-up. Jamie was the best player they had. A natural, Coach Russell said. Pressure never rattled ones who never felt the pressure and the ones who figured out how to deal with it. Jamie was the first kind. Meg was trying hard to be the second.

She took a deep breath and reviewed her stance. Toes slightly out, knees slightly bent. Weight on the balls of the feet. Hands down, glove facing the batter. Rock forward slightly on each pitch.

The first pitch sped toward home plate. Meg rocked forward and tried to remember what to do. A part of her mind registered the *whang* of the bat hitting the ball. As the batter sprinted for first base, the ball rocketed toward her.

It was to her left, but before she even began to move, the ball sped by her into center field. Runner on third base. Error to the shortstop.

I'll do better at bat, Meg thought. I'll get a hit.

But it didn't work out that way. She didn't get a hit all day. She struck out twice, popped out once, and was thrown out on a weak grounder. And she made another error in the field. Coach Russell wanted to see her after the game.

He sat behind his desk in his cubbyhole of an office, a kind-faced man with spiky hair the exact color of the infield dirt. Right now the expression on his face was unreadable.

"Tough day, Meg," he said quietly as he marked a chart with a stubby pencil. He looked up at her as she stood nervously holding her Falcons cap in front of her like a shield. "This isn't life or death, you know," he went on. "It's just a game and it's supposed to be fun. But I've got to tell you, some of the kids who saw you play the way you did today will think *they* should be on the team instead of you."

Meg stood silent, miserable.

"You know why I picked you for the team, Meg?" She shook her head. "Because you have good skills and natural talent. You're a hard worker and you know the game. You *love* the game. I'm on your side. I've got two daughters younger than you. I think it would be great if you could be a trailblazer so they could play without all this fuss about being a girl." He cleared his throat and looked down at his hands.

"I've got no choice here, Meg. If you don't improve in the next couple of games, I'll have to find a new shortstop."

There was nothing to say. She turned to go, unshed tears burning her eyes.

"Meg!"

She couldn't turn around and let him see her tear-bright eyes, but she stood still to listen, her damp hand clutching the doorknob.

"I just want you to know I think you've got more natural talent than any other player on the team. I'm just an electrician who likes coaching baseball, but that's what I think."

She nodded and went out. It was the longest conversation she'd ever had with Coach Russell, and she hadn't said a word.

Her mother wasn't much help. She had been the Jamie Ferguson kind of champion, the kind who never feels the pressure. "You can't let it get to you, Meggie," she said. "You try too hard. Just relax more and have some fun."

She was having misery. She was having panic. She was definitely *not* having fun.

In the living room Meg found her dad trying to get Charles to put a puzzle together. Charles was grunting. That meant he'd be crying in a minute.

"Sing 'Yuckee Doodoo,'" Meg suggested.

"Huh?" Her dad gave her a blank look.

Meg sang, Charles grinned, and fit a puzzle piece into its slot.

"Dad?"

"Mmm?"

"Ever play any baseball?

He laughed. "Nope. Your mom's the athlete in the family. But I'll tell you a deep, dark secret if you promise not to laugh."

"Promise."

"When I was in college, you had to have some physical education credits. You could take anything you wanted, so I took fencing."

"You're kidding. You mean you wore those white ninja outfits and fought with swords?"

"Foils, actually, but, yeah, that's the idea. The whole thing appealed to my romantic nature. I was crazy about it. The problem was that I was so bad, I was on the verge of flunking."

"So did you flunk?"

"No. My instructor was terrified that if he flunked me, he'd just be stuck with me again the next semester. So he gave me some advice. He said when he was learning, he used to sing the French national anthem to himself. It helped him forget all the rules and procedures and just *fence*."

"Did it work?"

"Not his song. I used 'Jabberwocky.'"

He jumped up and waved an imaginary foil.

"'Twas brillig"—*thrust*—"and the slithy toves"—*thrust*—"did gyre"—*thrust*—"and gimble"—*thrust*—"in the wabe." *Thrust, flourish.*

He stopped and grinned down at Meg. "It actually helped. I wound up with C, and my poor instructor never had to deal with me again."

Meg considered. "I see your point. I get tangled up worrying about technique. But I don't know 'Jabberwocky.'"

"No problem. What do you know inside out so you don't have to think about it?"

Meg looked at Charles. "'Yuckee Doodoo.'"

She was in her shortstop's crouch and she was singing. "Yankee Doodle went to town, a-riding on a pony, stuck a feather in his cap and called it macaroni. Yankee Doodle, keep it up—"

Whap! The bat slammed into Meg's glove. "Mind the music and the step—"

She hauled the ball out of her glove and hurled it to first base. "And with the girls be handy!"

The batter was trotting back to the dugout. Out at first. By a mile.

Jamie Ferguson glanced over and gave her a thumbs-up. Coach Russell was smiling. Meg started in on the second verse as the next batter stepped up to the plate.

Great-Grandmother's Secret

BY JEAN LEJCHER

William ran up the steps, past Great-Grandmother sitting on the porch swing.

"Hi, Gram. I'm going to hang our flag."

Tap, tap, tap, bounced Great-Grandmother's wooden cane—her way of talking since she'd had her stroke.

William kissed her cheek. He missed visiting with Gram. Now he could only guess what she was trying to say through her cane's tapping. Mostly her thoughts were a mystery.

He rushed through the doorway to the hall closet, where he rummaged among coats and jackets. He checked the closet floor, pushing around shoes, boxes, and a scuffed, brown leather suitcase, in search of the flag his mother hung every Fourth of July.

"Where is that flag?" William asked. He turned toward the screen door, watching Gram as she rocked back and forth. A hanky peeked from her sleeve, and in her hand she held an old picture of Great-Grandfather. Ever since he'd died two years ago, Gram carried the picture with her wherever she went.

William pushed against a familiar shape: the pole, without the flag, fell forward.

"What are you looking for?" asked William's mother from the kitchen doorway.

"Where's the flag? I want to hang our flag and be patriotic like everyone else," replied William. He pointed out the window to the neighbors' houses and yards and to cars diving by with flags flying from antennas.

William's mother set down her towel. "That's exactly what I've been thinking, except there is one problem. The flag we used last summer was frayed and worn, so I took it to the American Legion. The collect old flags and dispose of them properly."

Tap, tap, tap, jumped Great-Grandmother's cane.

"Then we'll get a new flag. Come on, let's go right now," said William.

Williams's mother placed her hand on his shoulder. "I've called all over. Everyone's had the same thought, and there are no flags left in the stores. It may take up to two weeks to get one."

"It's not fair! I want to be patriotic, too," said William.

Tap, tap, tap, hopped Great-Grandmother's cane.

"I'll make my own flag," said William. He went to the desk and took out paper and markers and drew the stars and stripes of the American flag. Halfway through his coloring, the red marker ran dry. He finished the remaining red stripes with a crayon.

William took his paper flag out to the porch. "Gram, I made a flag," he said, "but it looks terrible. The red stripes on top are brighter than the ones on the bottom. And I went outside the lines a few times." He crunched the paper into a ball and swung his arm out to throw it. Instead he bumped Great-Grandmother's hand, and the picture flew out, hitting the floor and shattering the glass.

William's eyes grew wide. He knelt at Great-Grandmother's feet holding Great-Grandfather's picture. Tears threatened as he whispered, "I'm sorry, Gram"

William picked up pieces of the glass off the floor. From around the picture's frame, he carefully cleaned away the sharp edges. Then he lifted Great-Grandmother's hand and curled her fingers gently around the picture.

Tap, tap, tap, danced Great-Grandmother's cane, harder than before.

"I'm sorry. I didn't mean to—" Before William could finish, Great-Grandmother pushed the picture back toward him.

Tap, tap, tap.

"I...I cleaned it the best I could, " said William. Then, for the first time, he looked closely at the black-and-white picture. Great-Grandmother wore her wedding dress, and Great-Grandfather, his army uniform. She leaned over and pointed to the brown leather suitcase at Great-Grandfather's foot. "The suitcase! It's the one in the closet," said William.

Tap, tap, tap.

"You want the suitcase?" asked William. He fetched the suitcase, then sat next to Great-Grandmother. He flipped the latches and lifted its cover, staring at the triangular object inside. He slowly realized what it was—an American flag.

William remembered that the flag had covered Great-Grandfather's casket at the funeral. He remembered the white-gloved color guard folding the flag, then presenting it to Great-Grandmother.

Tap, tap, tap.

"I can't. I couldn't" stammered William.

"Yes you can, William," said he mother from the doorway. "Gram wouldn't have showed you how to find it if she didn't want you to fly the flag."

William lifted it from the suitcase. Together, he and his mother unfolded it. She shook out the wrinkles and held the pole while William fastened the flag to it.

When the flag was hung, all three of them watched as the flag caught the breeze and unfurled, dancing up and away from the house.

Uncle Sam and Old Glory: Symbols of America

BY DELNO C. WEST AND JEAN M. WEST

The AMERICAN FLAG

Every morning, millions of children in classrooms across America stand with their hands over their hearts and say these words: "I pledge allegiance to the flag of the United States of America, and to the Republic for which it stands, one nation under God, indivisible, with liberty and justice for all." They address these words to the American flag, which is sometimes called the "Stars and Stripes," "Old Glory," or the "Star-Spangled Banner."

In July 1775, George Washington, the new commander of the Continental Army, thought a special flag should be made to represent all the colonies who were rebelling against the British government. So the Continental Congress, the government at the time, came up with a design and approved it on June 14, 1777. Most people think that General Washington then asked a Philadelphia seamstress named Betsy Ross to sew the first flag, but no one really knows if this is true.

The red, white, and blue colors and the stars and stripes are symbols of the American spirit. White stands for liberty, red for courage, and blue symbolizes loyalty. Every aspect of the flag's design stands for an important idea too.

The thirteen red and white stripes represent the original thirteen colonies. On the early flags, stripes were added as well as stars when new states entered the Union. The real "Star Spangled Banner" had fifteen stripes and fifteen stars. Since then, only stars have been added to symbolize additional states.

Many people have died protecting our country, and the flag reminds many of us of all the great things about America for which people were willing to give their lives. This feeling of love for our country is called "patriotism."

Sometimes people use the flag to protest when they disagree with government actions. They burn the flag, walk on it, or hang it upside down. This has led groups of Americans to fight one another, as each group uses the American flag to symbolize its own beliefs.

Ode To Family Photographs

BY GARY SOTO

This is the pond, and these are my feet.
This is the rooster, and this is more of my feet.

Mamá was never good at pictures.

This is a statue of a famous general who lost an arm,
And this is me with my head cut off.

This is a trash can chained to a gate,
This is my father with his eyes half-closed.

This is a photograph of my sister
And a giraffe looking over her shoulder.

This is our car's front bumper.
This is a bird with a pretzel in its beak.
This is my brother Pedro standing on one leg on a rock,
With a smear of chocolate on his face.

Mamá sneezed when she looked
Behind the camera: the snapshots are blurry,
The angles dizzy as a spin on a merry-go-round.

But we had fun when Mamá picked up the camera.
How can I tell?
Each of us is laughing hard.
Can you see? I have candy in my mouth.

"Ode to Family Photographs" from *Neighborhood Odes*, copyright ©
1992 by Gary Soto, reprinted by permission of Harcourt, Inc.

Happy Birthday, Mother Dearest

BY JACK PRELUTSKY

Happy birthday, Mother dearest,
we made breakfast just for you,
a watermelon omelette,
and a dish of popcorn too,
a cup of milk and sugar,
and a slice of blackened toast,
happy birthday, Mother dearest,
you're the one we love the most.

Seeing All My Family

BY CLAIRE SALAMA

Seeing all my family together
at special occasions
is a brilliant firework show
going off.
Grandma is a sparkler,
Grandad is golden rain
making us brighter.
My cousins
are Catherine Wheels.
My dad is a banger
because he always talks too loud.
The best one of all
that lights up the sky
so everyone stares
is my mum
the incredible blast of sparkle
the rocket.
Every time we meet,
it always has the same effect
our family firework show.

"Seeing All My Family" by Claire Salama from *Wondercrump 3* edited
by Jennifer Curry, published by Red Fox. Reprinted by permission of
The Random House Group Ltd.

B is for Buckaroo:
A Cowboy Alphabet

WRITTEN BY LOUISE DOAK WHITNEY & GLEAVES WHITNEY

Andalusia begins with an A—Spanish land that's far away. It's where our story begins of the colorful cowboy way.

B is for the Buckaroo, who's a cowboy through and through. These broncobusters you'll often see riding on horseback, yelling "Whoopee!"

Chuck wagon starts with the letter C. It's the place where cowboys like to be, to enjoy tasty vittles and a cup of coffee, and tell tall tales out on the prairie.

D is for the Dally the drovers like to make, when they need a little dogie to put on the brake!

E is for the Endless plains stretching as far as the eye can see. For cowboys and cattle it was home, the land that gave them room to roam.

F is for the Frying Pan—A ranch with a funny name. It's where the barbed wire fence began and Joseph Glidden earned his fame.

G is for all the Gear that cowboys like to wear—Boots, hats, jeans, and chaps as they work and ride the frontier.

Have you ever heard of the "Stetson," the "Ten Gallon," or the "Boss of the Plains"? Hats are our letter H—Keeping off the sun, rain, and snow. With a tall crown and wide brim, they sure do make a show.

Iron starts with the letter I, white hot from the fire. An iron horseshoe and iron brand the blacksmith forges by hand.

Jinglebob begins with the letter J—It's the little bell on a spur, jingling, jangling all day, especially when cowboys dance and play.

King Ranch begins with the letter K. It's where American ranching began. To learn about the cowboy way, visit this spread if you can.

Now let's lasso some L words. . . . L is for Lariat or Lasso, a loop of rope coiled just so. Swing it wide or swing it low. Hook those longhorns and yell "Whoa!"

Mesteño starts with the letter M—It's a mustang, a horse wild and free. Hard work and time will tame it so a faithful partner it can be.

Under the moonlit, starry night, rode the Night herd, our letter N. Cowboys keeping watch over the cattle would sometimes nod off in the saddle!

Annie Oakley is the letter O, the star of Buffalo Bill's Wild West Show. "Little Sure Shot" was her nickname—Her sharp shooting brought her fame.

Pecos Bill starts with the letter P. The original cowboy legend was he. He rode a cyclone without a saddle and sang songs to quiet the cattle.

Q is for the Quarter horse that a cowboy loves to ride. Old Sorrel was the first of the breed, with a fast and sturdy stride.

Riding the bulls or roping calves, let's round up an R for Rodeo. Cowboy clowns and bucking broncos put on a ripsnortin' show!

S stands for Saddle with a horn, cinch, and cantle. It's a throne on a horse for a cowboy, of course!

T is for the many Trails, used to herd cattle to the rails. With names like Goodnight and Santa Fe, they remain a legend to this day.

Union Pacific is the train that starts with the letter U. Listen for the lonely whistle as it crosses the plains—choo choo!

Vaquero starts with the letter V—A Spanish cowboy was he. Knowing how to rope and ride, he was the first of the cowboy pride.

W is for Will Rogers, the king of cowboy philosophers. He did fancy tricks with his lassos to thrill kids at the *Wild West Show!*

X is for the ranch called the XIT, bigger than any other you'll see. It's also a famous brand known for miles across the land.

Yodeling starts with the letter Y—Cowboys crooning way up high. Tunes that'll get your toes a tappin' and keep both your hands a clappin'.

At last we come to Zane Grey, whose first name starts with a Z. He wrote stories about cowboys to be enjoyed by you and me.

Cowboy: An Album

BY LINDA GRANFIELD

A cowboy poet once remarked, "In some ways, we're born a hundred years too late. In other ways, we're a reminder of something in danger of being lost." The cowboy of the Old West is certainly a part of the world's legends, but he is not in danger of being forgotten.

There are still plenty of cattle ranches around the world—in North America, Australia, and South America, for instance. Cowboys still work hard during spring calving season, during the roundup and branding times, and during the cold winter months at the ranch. Often ranches are operated by the third or fourth generation of the same cowboy family.

But times have changed too. The cowboy's rope may be nylon, not rawhide. While the horse remains the favorite mode of transportation, a visitor to a modern ranch can also find cowboys carrying out their daily chores on snowmobiles, in trucks, and in helicopters. Computers have entered the front offices of the world's ranches. Ranch lands are subdivided or rented out as cattle prices rise and fall, and owners struggle to make a living.

All over the world, condominiums and modern subdivisions are creeping into the cowboy's workplace. The loud engines of recreational vehicles terrorize the cattle and ruin good grazing land. Visitors on foot and on horseback cause more damage.

So why do cattlemen continue to ranch? Why do cowboys carry on their riding and roping? Many agree that they keep working because of their pride in the cowboy tradition. The cowboy life represents to them honesty, independence, a work ethic, and a respect for the land that they wish to pass down to their children. These truths are not buried in the broken buildings of western ghost towns, not lost in the romantic visions offered up in films. They are very much alive wherever the cowboy performs his duties, in spite of, and alongside of, the modern world.

Bringing the Light

BY ELIZABETH GAWLIK

Karin watched the children playing and heard their strange mix of words in Spanish and Quechua. Sometimes she understood their shouts, "¡Apúrate! Hurry!" or "¡Espérame! Wait for me!" But most of the time their cries blended together, and she didn't know whether they were speaking Spanish, Quechua, or a language all their own. Today, though, she needed to talk to them. She needed to find the things for Lucia soon, because time was running out.

It was already December twelfth, and before tomorrow she needed candles, a white robe, a red sash, and a crown of evergreen branches. As the daughter in family, she had the job of bringing the light on the longest night of winter. Of course, in this strange place there was no sign of winter, just heavy rain. But, still, she just had to make sure that their most important tradition from home didn't disappear. They had left behind so many other things when they moved from Sweden to this tiny South American village in the mountains of Peru.

Karin thought of her family's Saint Lucia tradition. She loved the white robe and red sash that she wore every year. She would carefully place the fir wreath with the lighted candles on her head and bring delicious treats to the family on the morning of the celebration. This always reminded her of the beautiful story of Saint Lucia, who had brought food to the poor and light to the blind.

Now that Karin's family had come here as missionaries, the Lucia tradition simply had to come with them.

Karin knew there was a market, but she did not know how to find it. She saw a boy sitting by himself in the dirty street, playing with a toy. He looked about eight years old, just a little younger than Karin. She tried one of her Spanish words. "*¿Mercado?*" she asked. The boy pointed down one of the streets. "*Allá.*" The market was somewhere in the direction he was pointing. But how far was it? She tried another word: "*¿Lejos?*" The boy shook his head. It wasn't far. Karin still looked confused, so the boy got up and started walking in the direction he'd pointed. He motioned for Karin to follow him.

She gathered up her courage and walked down the street. Suddenly there came the sound of many hoofs, and the boy pulled Karin over to the wall. A herd of llamas was coming, driven by a boy in a multicolored poncho with a big, black hat. He smiled at Karin. As the llamas passed, an oddly familiar scent hit her. The animals smelled like the fields outside Stockholm at planting time. Karin had never liked that smell at home, but here it was almost comforting.

When they reached the market, she smiled at the boy to show her thanks, and he turned back. Karin walked up to the first market stall, but she didn't know what they were selling. She asked, "*¿Luz?* Light?" but the women didn't understand her, so she went on. Finally she came to a stall where a young woman was sitting. Again she asked, "*¿Luz?*" The woman smiled and handed Karin something that looked a little like a candle.

It wasn't like the candles at home, but it would do. "*¿Más?*" the woman asked her, and Karin nodded, showing that she wanted more. The young woman took out several more candles. Karin gave the woman some coins and walked on.

Now she had the light, but she needed so much more. Where could she find a white robe? None of the people here wore light clothing, maybe because of all the mud. It must be hard to wash their clothes in the river as she had seen the women do.

Karin looked around at all the dark blankets and almost began to cry. One of the women, seeing that Karin was upset, tried to comfort her, murmuring words in Quechua. Karin realized the woman wanted to know what was wrong. She pointed at one of the blankets and asked, "*¿Blanco?*" The woman shook her head. No, she had no white blankets. She showed Karin one that was light brown with red stripes. Karin thought about it. Maybe the red stripes would work instead of the sash. It would be different, but it might be pretty.

Next she needed some evergreen branches, but there were no evergreens here. In fact, Karin had never even seen a tree in the village. She needed the woman's help again. She used another word. "*¿Árbol?*" she asked. The woman pointed to a group of scraggly-looking plants. Karin couldn't believe those were trees. She tried again, but the woman just pointed to the same place. Karin walked to the spot and saw that, after all, these were trees.

Or, at least, they had some strange branches and thick green leaves. They weren't at all like evergreens, but they were the best Karin could find. She broke off one of the thinnest branches and put it in the blanket with the candles.

The next morning, Karin's parents woke to an unexpected sound. Karin walked slowly into their room, singing the traditional Lucia song, *"Natten går tunga fjät . . ."* in her lovely voice. She was wrapped in the Peruvian blanket, the candles were stuck in her crown of green leaves, and she carried a tray with hot chocolate.

Her father gasped. "My little Karin," he exclaimed, "you are beautiful! You have brought us our old home in the clothing of the new. This is a perfect surprise."

Karin smiled. Maybe Lucia didn't need to stay in Sweden. Maybe she could live in South America too.